Different Schools for a Different World

Scott McLeod
Dean Shareski

Solution Tree | Press

555 North Morton Street
Bloomington, IN 47404
800.733.6786 (toll free) / 812.336.7700
FAX: 812.336.7790

email: info@SolutionTree.com
SolutionTree.com

Printed in the United States of America

21   20   19   18   17   1   2   3   4   5

Library of Congress Cataloging-in-Publication Data

Names: McLeod, Scott, 1968- author. | Shareski, Dean, author.
Title: Different schools for a different world / Scott McLeod and Dean
  Shareski.
Description: Bloomington, IN : Solution Tree Press, 2017. | Series: Solutions
  series | Includes bibliographical references.
Identifiers: LCCN 2017016974 | ISBN 9781943874101 (perfect bound)
Subjects: LCSH: Educational change--United States. | Education--Aims and
  objectives--United States. | Educational accountability--United States. |
  Comparative education.
Classification: LCC LA217.2 .M3996 2017 | DDC 370.973--dc23 LC record available at
https://lccn.loc.gov/2017016974

Solution Tree
Jeffrey C. Jones, CEO
Edmund M. Ackerman, President

Solution Tree Press
President and Publisher: Douglas M. Rife
Editorial Director: Sarah Payne-Mills
Managing Production Editor: Caroline Cascio
Senior Production Editor: Tara Perkins
Senior Editor: Amy Rubenstein
Proofreader: Evie Madsen
Text Designer: Rian Anderson
Compositor: Laura Cox
Cover Designer: Laura Cox
Editorial Assistants: Jessi Finn and Kendra Slayton

To Betsy, Isabel, Lucas, and Colin, who put up with my shenanigans and without whom everything would be meaningless.

—Scott

To Paula and all those kids and their mates, who still don't know exactly what their husband and father does for a living.

—Dean

Acknowledgments

Solution Tree Press would like to thank the following reviewers:

Kevin Doerfler
Assistant Principal
Portage West Middle School
Portage, Michigan

Michael Roberts
Principal
Desert View Elementary School
Hermiston, Oregon

Bo Ryan
Principal
Greater Hartford Academy of the Arts Magnet Middle School
Hartford, Connecticut

Kristy Venne
Assistant Principal
Dublin Jerome High School
Dublin, Ohio

Table of Contents

About the Authors

 **Scott McLeod**, an associate professor of educational leadership at the University of Colorado Denver, is widely recognized as one of the United States' leading experts in preK–12 school technology leadership. He is the founding director of the University Council for Educational Administration's Center for the Advanced Study of Technology Leadership in Education, the only U.S. university center dedicated to the technology needs of school administrators. He is co-creator of the *Did You Know? (Shift Happens)* video series and the trudacot (technology-rich unit design and classroom observation template) technology integration discussion protocol.

Scott has worked with several hundred schools, districts, universities, and other organizations and has received numerous awards for his technology leadership work, including the 2016 Award for Outstanding Leadership from the International Society for Technology in Education (ISTE). In 2015, he was one of three finalists to be the director of the Iowa Department of Education. In 2011, he was a visiting faculty fellow at the University of Canterbury in New Zealand. Scott was one of the pivotal figures in Iowa's grassroots one-to-one computing movement, which has resulted in more than 220 school districts providing their students with powerful learning devices, and founded the annual Iowa one-to-one Institute and EdCampIowa.

Scott blogs regularly about technology leadership and shares numerous resources through his Digital Leadership Daily SMS service. Scott is a frequent keynote speaker and workshop facilitator at regional, state, national, and international conferences. He has written 170 articles and other publications and is the co-editor of *What School Leaders Need to Know About Digital Technologies and Social Media*.

To learn more about Scott's work, visit his blog, *Dangerously Irrelevant* (http://dangerouslyirrelevant.org), or follow @mcleod on Twitter.

Dean Shareski is the community manager for Discovery Education Canada. He taught grades 1–8 for fourteen years and spent nine years as a digital learning consultant for Prairie South School Division in Moose Jaw, Saskatchewan. In addition, he has taught and designed courses both at the University of Regina in Saskatchewan and at Wilkes University in Pennsylvania.

Dean's blog, *Ideas and Thoughts*, consistently ranks among the top educational blogs. He also blogs for *Tech and Learning* and *The Huffington Post*. In 2010, he won the International Society for Technology in Education (ISTE) Award for Outstanding Leader of the Year.

Dean has had the opportunity to speak to a variety of education audiences within the United States and Canada as well as outside North America. He believes humor and humility go a long way in supporting and advocating transformational practices in teaching and learning. More important, his efforts to promote joyful learning and working environments remain his greatest passion.

He holds a master's degree in educational technology from the University of Saskatchewan. Dean has been married to his wife Paula for more than thirty years, and together they celebrate their four children and their families. When not teaching and sharing, you might find Dean on a golf course.

To learn more about Dean's work, visit his blog, *Ideas and Thoughts* (http://ideasandthoughts.org), or follow @shareski on Twitter.

To book Scott McLeod or Dean Shareski for professional development, contact pd@SolutionTree.com.

Foreword

By William M. Ferriter

Can I ask you a tough question? How many students in your classrooms are truly satisfied with the learning spaces you have created for them? If your kids reflect the national average, the answer is bound to be discouraging. Fewer than four in ten high schoolers report being engaged in their classes, and students often list boredom as the primary reason for dropping out of school (Busteed, 2013). Over 70 percent of students who don't graduate report having lost interest by ninth grade and, worse yet, the majority of dropouts are convinced that motivation is all that prevented them from earning a diploma (Azzam, 2007).

These numbers are troubling for anyone passionate about schools. They indicate systemic failure on the part of practitioners to inspire learners and warn us of the immediate need to transform education—a warning that school leadership expert and series contributor Scott McLeod (2014) issues:

> If we truly care about preparing kids for life and work success—*we need schools to be different.* If economic success increasingly means moving away from routine cognitive work, schools need to also move in that direction. If our analog, ink-on-paper information landscapes outside of school have been superseded by environments that are digital and online and hyperconnected and mobile, our information landscapes inside of school also should reflect those shifts. If our students' extracurricular learning opportunities often are richer and deeper than what they experience in their formal educational settings, it is time for us to catch up.

Scott is right, isn't he? Our schools really do need to catch up if they are going to remain relevant in a world where learning is more important than schooling—and catching up can only start when we are willing to rethink everything. We need to push aside the current norms defining education—that teachers are to govern, direct, and evaluate student work; that mastering content detailed in predetermined curricula is the best indicator of student success; that assessment and remediation are more important than feedback and reflection; that the primary reason for investing in tools and technologies is to improve on existing practices. It's time to implement notions that better reflect the complexity of the world in which we live.

That is the origin of this series. It is my attempt to give a handful of the most progressive educators that I know a forum for detailing what they believe it will take to *make schools different*. Each book encourages readers to question their core beliefs about what meaningful teaching and learning look like in action. More important, each title provides readers with practical steps and strategies for reimagining their day-to-day practices. Here's your challenge: no matter how unconventional ideas, steps, and strategies may seem at first, and no matter how uncomfortable they make you feel, find a way to take action. There is no other way to create the learning spaces that your students deserve.

Introduction

Make school different.
—Seth Godin

In 1983, the U.S. National Commission on Excellence in Education issued a landmark report. The report, titled *A Nation at Risk*, includes the following statements:

> Our once unchallenged preeminence in commerce, industry, science, and technological innovation is being overtaken by competitors throughout the world. . . . If an unfriendly foreign power had attempted to impose on America the mediocre educational performance that exists today, we might well have viewed it as an act of war. . . . We have . . . squandered the gains in student achievement made in the wake of the Sputnik challenge. . . . We have, in effect, been committing an act of unthinking, unilateral educational disarmament. (p. 5)

These alarmist statements echoed the fears of previous generations that U.S. students were unprepared for the world around them. They also revitalized the notion that U.S. students were woefully inadequate compared to their international peers, a tale that has been told for decade after decade regardless of the United States' economic progress or the happiness and well-being of its citizens.

In the decades since *A Nation at Risk*, reports of the United States' imminent educational demise have continued. Business RoundTable (2005) postulates that "the United States is in a fierce contest with other nations . . . but other countries are demonstrating a greater commitment to building their brainpower" (p. 1). Similarly, the New Commission on the Skills of the American Workforce (2006) states: "Whereas for most of the 20th century the United States could take pride in having the best-educated workforce in the world, that is no longer true. Over the past 30 years, one country after another has surpassed us" (p. 4). And the highly respected National Academy of Science (2007) says that "without a renewed effort to bolster the foundations of our competitiveness, we can expect to lose our privileged position. For the first time in generations, the nation's children could face poorer prospects than their parents and grandparents did" (p. 13).

The United States (as well as Canada) is not alone in this alarmism over assessment results. Just as sports enthusiasts look over league tables and box scores every morning, so too do many national governments pore over the minute details and rankings of their own tests and the Programme for International Student Assessment (PISA). Fearmongering and hand-wringing about education have become international pastimes.

That fear has narrowed and impoverished our views of learning and teaching. We ratchet up curriculum standards and devise cut scores based on political considerations rather than educational outcomes (for an example, see Bracey, 2009). We come up with standardized test after standardized test after standardized test for our students. It's not enough to have both end-of-year grade-level and graduation exams: we must also have numerous benchmarking tests during the year to make sure that students are on track for those final exams. We try to attach numeric data to everything we do, including not just academic performance but also social and emotional growth. We try to tie teacher evaluations to these student assessment results, which leads to such farces as physical education teachers facing sanctions because of mathematics scores for students they don't even teach.

The Relevance Gap

As nations perceive their students are falling behind international peers and make specious links to national economic well-being, they focus on narrow academic achievement gaps rather than on empowering students broadly for life success. But, as David N. Perkins (2014) notes:

> The achievement gap asks, "Are students achieving X?" whereas the relevance gap asks, "Is X going to matter to the lives learners are likely to live?" If X is good mastery of reading and writing, both questions earn a big yes! Skilled, fluent, and engaged reading and writing mark both a challenging gap and a high-payoff attainment. That knowledge goes somewhere! However, if X is quadratic equations, the answers don't match. Mastering quadratic equations is challenging, but these equations are not so lifeworthy. Now fill in X with any of the thousands of topics that make up the typical content curriculum. Very often, these topics present significant challenges of achievement but with little return on investment in learners' lives. Here's the problem: the achievement gap is much more concerned with mastering content than with providing lifeworthy content. . . . The achievement gap is all about doing the same thing better. . . . The relevance gap asks us to reconsider deeply what schools teach in the first place. (p. 10)

It's no wonder engagement, educator morale, teacher recruitment and retention, and parent satisfaction with schools are so low—and why little or no academic improvement seems to result (Brown, 2015). As Perkins (2014) asks, "What did you learn during your first twelve years of education that matters in your life today?" (p. 10). For many, the answer is "not as much as schools hope." This disconnect that exists for so many of our graduates is just one of the many reasons we believe schools need to be different.

Arguments for Why Schools Need to Be Different

In this book, we outline six key arguments for why schools need to be different. These are not the only six arguments one could make but are important ones that address our changing, increasingly connected world—and how most of our classrooms fail to change in response to it. If political and school leaders—whom we consider the major audiences for this book, along with teachers, concerned parents, and anyone with a stake in the future of education—want to adapt learning and teaching environments to the demands of the 21st century, it is imperative that they understand the real challenges that future graduates will face. To recognize where our educational policymaking conversations have gone wrong, we have to zoom out of the day-to-day realities of schools and instead look at the societal contexts in which our school systems operate. If we hope to prepare our students and graduates for the world around them, we must start by observing and understanding what that world is actually like.

Our six arguments for making schools different are based on the following observations, each of which corresponds to the first six chapters.

1. Our information landscape is becoming incredibly complex and students need the skills to navigate it effectively.
2. Automation and global hypercompetition increasingly define the economy that our graduates are entering.
3. The role of teachers as exclusive purveyors of information is obsolete.
4. The tasks we ask students to perform are often undemanding and tedious, leading to boredom and a lack of critical thinking.
5. Schools are doing too little to create a culture of educational innovation that can respond to evolving student needs.
6. The digital tools students will require for future success are too often unavailable to traditionally disadvantaged groups.

Many of the schools that are successfully tackling these problems and ensuring relevance for students are what the Hewlett Foundation (2017) calls *deeper learning schools*. In chapter 7, we examine their effectiveness and highlight the practices of a few exemplar deeper learning schools.

[handwritten margin note: Which students do these give to?]

Four Big Shifts and Ten Building Blocks

These deeper learning schools and other innovative educational organizations are serious about addressing this book's six arguments head-on. They recognize that if we want different learning and life outcomes for students, we have to design for them. Accordingly, deeper learning schools make most (and usually all) of the following four big shifts in their approaches to schooling.

1. **Higher-level thinking:** The shift from an overwhelming emphasis on lower-level-thinking tasks, such as factual recall and procedural regurgitation, to tasks of greater cognitive complexity, such as creativity, critical thinking, problem solving, and effective communication and collaboration. In other words, this shift asks students to live more often on the upper levels of Benjamin S. Bloom's (1956) taxonomy (or Norman L. Webb's [2002] Depth of Knowledge model) than the lower ones. The shift away from lower-level thinking helps foster graduates' citizenship skills, economic and college success, and life readiness.

2. **Student agency:** The shift from classrooms that teachers overwhelmingly control to learning environments that enable greater student agency over what, how, when, where, who with, and why they learn. Student agency allows for greater personalization, individualization, and differentiation of the learning process. As a result, student disengagement diminishes because students have greater autonomy and ownership over more of their learning.

3. **Authentic work:** The shift from isolated academic work to environments that provide students opportunities to engage with and contribute to local, national, and international interdisciplinary learning communities. This shift supports students' motivation by helping them see direct connections between their learning and the world around them, and identify the content's relevance to their future lives. It more directly connects students' learning activities to the societal innovations that surround them, enabling schools' instruction and curricula to be more contemporary.

4. **Technology infusion:** The shift from local classrooms that are largely based on pens and pencils, notebook paper, ring binders, and printed textbooks to globally connected learning spaces that are deeply and richly technology driven. The new affordances of mobile computing devices and online environments allow the first three shifts mentioned here to move into high gear. Robust technology integration efforts also combat equity concerns, allow students to master current information landscapes, and increase relevance to rapid, technology-driven societal innovations.

Deeper learning schools tend to use a common set of building blocks to form the foundation of their work. These building blocks vary in form, depth, and intensity depending on the classroom or school model, but together they foster the four big shifts that define innovative schools. Not all these building blocks are present in every deeper learning school, but most deeper learning school models incorporate at least a few. In no particular order, they are:

- **Project- and inquiry-based learning environments** that emphasize greater student agency and the active application of cognitively complex thinking, communication, and collaboration skills

- **Authentic, real-world work** students derive from community projects, internships, digital simulations, and other learning experiences

- **Competency-based education and standards-based grading** that shift the focus of assessment from seat time to learning mastery

- **One-to-one computing initiatives** (and concurrent Internet bandwidth upgrades) that give students access both to digital learning devices and to the world's information, individuals, and organizations

- **Digital and online information resources**, often including open-access resources

- **Online communities of interest** that supplement and augment more traditional learning communities

- **Adaptive software and data systems** (and accompanying organizational models) that facilitate greater individualization of learning content and pace

- **Alternative credentialing mechanisms** that enable individuals to quickly reskill for and adapt to rapidly evolving workforce needs and economic demands

- **Flexible scheduling** that moves students away from fifty-minute chunks of time—and a prescribed number of hours and days in a prescribed location—and toward opportunities to learn longer, deeper, and in more places about important life skills and concepts

- **Redesigned learning spaces** that accommodate flexible, student-centered grouping and learning tasks rather than classroom spaces that the needs of instructors or janitors dictate

Although these building blocks are presented here as separate items, they usually work in coordination to create qualitatively different learning experiences for students. The combinations a deeper learning school chooses—and the depth of their implementation—form that school's unique character.

Our Message

The intent of this book is not to denigrate the efforts of the numerous sincere and dedicated educators who are trying the best they can to serve students well within traditional school systems. We're both passionate advocates for schools, educators, and students; we both have long histories in the public education system; and we've both been vocal proponents of powerful learning, student and teacher rights, and adequate school supports and funding. But we also recognize that schools need to change (and if we've done our job right, by now you do too). We can't keep doing the same things that we have always done, nor can we continue to move at the frustratingly slow pace that we've seen so far.

The intent of this book is to recognize that despite our very best efforts, much of what we're doing in schools isn't working because it isn't relevant to the needs and demands of the world around us. For the most part, the problem lies not so much with our people but with the outdated systems that many of us are struggling to abandon. When societies shifted from an agricultural model to an industrial model, we responded by changing how we educated our young people. Now that our societies are shifting from an industrial model to a global information and innovation model, we need to change our approach to education yet again.

In some respects, the concerns in this book are no different from the concerns of the authors of *A Nation at Risk* and its many heirs. We also raise questions about the education that students experience in most of our schools. But our worries lie in completely different directions than poor performance on standardized tests, and our prescriptions bear little resemblance to the technocratic "solutions" that policymakers tend to prefer. We agree that schools need to change, but that change should have to do with a school's relevance, not just with its achievement scores. Complex problems don't get fixed with simplistic approaches.

The challenges that lie before us are too great—and the opportunities ahead are too powerful—for us to sit back and pretend that the status quo is adequate. We love schools. But we must change them in order to save them. However, the paths that we advocate for in this book so far have been unrealized on a large scale. And despite our eye on the future, we recognize that concerns regarding the relevance of contemporary education are timeless. We have always known what the goal of great, relevant learning looks like. Today, although we have more barriers to overcome, we also have more ways to achieve it.

Chapter 1
The Information Literacy Argument

Before newspapers, radio, and television, much of human information gathering was done on a one-to-one level, through local word of mouth. Eventually, this was supplanted by the beginnings of the analog information world, which started in earnest with ink on paper. Books, magazines, newspapers, fliers and leaflets, dictionaries, encyclopedias, folding maps, and other paper-based materials comprised the vast majority of our analog information space. Creating and distributing these materials was expensive, and large companies and international distribution channels emerged to move paper from point A to points B and C: think printing presses and delivery trucks and bookstores and newsstands and libraries.

We evolved a few other information channels as well. Telegraphs and telephones were great for point-to-point communication but didn't work very well for reaching the collective masses. Radio and television became ubiquitous, but as with their ink-on-paper counterparts, distribution was costly. Nearly every citizen could (and did) access radio and television content, but few had the resources to create and disseminate that content via transmission towers and network contracts.

Because of these distribution inefficiencies, information had only a few sources: those few commercial and government entities powerful or wealthy enough to afford a printing press, a broadcast station, or syndication rights could transmit it. In the analog world, nearly all of us were passive consumers of whatever information those entities decided that we should read, listen to, or watch.

These analog information channels are all still in existence as of the writing of this book. But digital and online channels—the so-called "cloud" that we can access through laptops, tablets, smartphones, and the Internet—are rapidly replacing them. This digital landscape creates new affordances and challenges for us as informed citizens. In this chapter, we will examine these new ways of communicating and accessing information, and consider how they offer new opportunities for collaboration.

New Ways of Communicating and Accessing Information

With digital information that moves at the speed of light, we can communicate in ways that are unhindered by geography and time. There are profound ramifications to this collapse of time and distance in normal human interactions. We regularly connect with individuals and communities across the planet, which urgently ratchets up our need to be globally aware citizens. In the 20th century, students often learned about people in other cultures through stereotypical presentations of those cultures' food and holidays. But in the digital world, our ability to interact with our peers in other countries requires us to go far beyond such minimal levels of awareness in order to achieve a deeper understanding and appreciation of who those peers are and how they think.

We connect more easily not only to people but also to pieces of information. In the analog world, only one person can own the original of a piece of information (such as a book, a document, or a map), and replicas may be inferior or expensive. In a digital world, however, we can all own the original, and often for free, with no degradation in quality even as quantity scales. These capabilities have facilitated unprecedented access to the world's sum of knowledge, but they've also stretched our conception of scarcity and put unbelievable stress on increasingly antiquated conceptions of copyright and intellectual property. They're also in direct conflict with most schools' thinking regarding collaboration, cheating, citation, and plagiarism.

Even as copyright faces challenges, we have new and vital abilities to be content creators. We can all have a voice, and we can all express that voice at a previously unimaginable scale. As *The Cluetrain Manifesto* notes way back in 2000, "There's a conversation going on today that wasn't happening [before]. . . . There are millions of threads in this conversation, but at the beginning and end of each one is a human being" (Levine, Locke, Searls, & Weinberger, 2000, p. 36). In the early 21st century, a twelve-year-old may be able to reach the same potential audience as a major media company. The implications of that for schools are enormous and almost completely unrealized.

Opportunities for Collaboration

We can not only communicate but also collaborate with others to create new value for our mutual benefit. We are witnessing the rapid rise not just of the cloud but also of the crowd. *Crowdsourcing* allows individuals who are geographically distributed but connected by their interests and passions to come together and, bit by bit, create enormous aggregated value. These include projects like Wikipedia and *The Huffington Post*, reviews on sites such as Amazon and TripAdvisor, marketplaces like Craigslist and Etsy, videos at BrickFilms and in Massachusetts Institute of Technology's Scratch programming community, tutorials at WikiHow and on YouTube, fan resources and stories at Wikia and FanFiction, business solutions generated at InnoCentive and 99designs, and citizen science projects at Galaxy Zoo and Project Noah—none of which would be possible in the analog world.

Crowdfunding, crowdsourcing's cousin, allows individuals to raise money directly from other people rather than through financial institutions. For example, the Kiva microlending service aggregates small financial contributions to help people in the developing world better themselves and their communities. Kickstarter, Indiegogo, and GoFundMe allow inventors, artists, and students to raise money for their projects without having to go to venture capital firms. DonorsChoose and Experiment.com allow teachers and scientists to crowdfund their needs. There are many more examples, and if you aren't familiar with the websites noted in these last two paragraphs, consider visiting some of them to understand our new crowd-related possibilities.

Is this shift in the way we share and relate to information unprecedented in history? According to Tom Standage (2013), today's new tools in many respects represent a return to humanity before the 20th century shift to mass media, back when ideas and information were primarily shared through individual word of mouth. In effect, many areas of today's information landscape now eliminate the authority of traditional media outlets, replacing them with individual producers who create and disseminate content via mobile phones, social media, and online platforms. Whereas our analog information landscape used to be centralized, limited by distance, and dominated by a few publishers and broadcasting networks, our new digital information landscape is decentralized, borderless, and highly distributed. Each of us is an information node and an information hub. Free content becomes a business model (Anderson, 2009; Jarvis, 2009). Privacy becomes a challenge.

This decentralization has already required corporations and politicians to be more transparent and accountable. It also has helped upend governments, as with the Arab Spring in 2010 and 2011, during which activists in the Middle East coordinated their actions and shared information through Twitter and other social media platforms in an attempt to overthrow the repressive leadership of several nations, including Egypt, Syria, and Libya.

In short, the power of information in our digital landscape is greater than ever before, yet our means for assessing the validity and authority of that information have changed. As a result, although the digital landscape empowers individuals as producers, it also requires them, as consumers, to master the skills of information filtering and critical thinking to a historically unprecedented degree.

There is no foreseeable future in which printed words—expensive and isolated—reassert their dominance over digital information—ubiquitous, cheap, and connected to the wider world. But in most classrooms, we still pretend otherwise. Schools serve many societal functions, but one of their primary roles is to help students master the dominant information landscape of their time. Giving students the skills to take advantage of and thrive in this new information landscape is one of the challenges that our schools must address.

Schools are supposed to prepare graduates with the knowledge to navigate the larger society outside school walls. Right now, we're largely failing on this front. To succeed, we must make schools different.

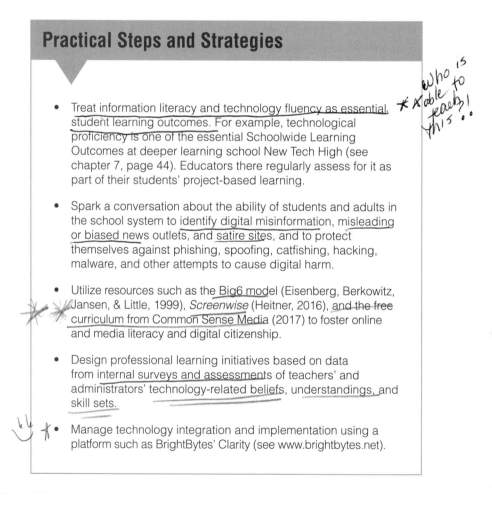

Practical Steps and Strategies

- Treat information literacy and technology fluency as essential student learning outcomes. For example, technological proficiency is one of the essential Schoolwide Learning Outcomes at deeper learning school New Tech High (see chapter 7, page 44). Educators there regularly assess for it as part of their students' project-based learning.

- Spark a conversation about the ability of students and adults in the school system to identify digital misinformation, misleading or biased news outlets, and satire sites, and to protect themselves against phishing, spoofing, catfishing, hacking, malware, and other attempts to cause digital harm.

- Utilize resources such as the Big6 model (Eisenberg, Berkowitz, Jansen, & Little, 1999), *Screenwise* (Heitner, 2016), and the free curriculum from Common Sense Media (2017) to foster online and media literacy and digital citizenship.

- Design professional learning initiatives based on data from internal surveys and assessments of teachers' and administrators' technology-related beliefs, understandings, and skill sets.

- Manage technology integration and implementation using a platform such as BrightBytes' Clarity (see www.brightbytes.net).

Chapter 2
The Economic Argument

Let's start with this basic premise: manufacturing jobs are not coming back. For a long time, in America and other developed countries, people with only a high school degree—or maybe not even that—could get a job at the local factory that included health benefits, personal leave, and a retirement pension. That salary also was high enough to raise a family and buy the occasional car, television, or vacation and to otherwise allow for a middle-class life. Those factories served as an economic safety valve for the general population, providing stable employment and boosting the well-being of tens of millions of families despite their fairly low levels of education. In this chapter, we reflect on the declining numbers of manufacturing jobs in developed countries and the ways in which automation influences both high- and low-skill jobs.

Disappearing Manufacturing Jobs in Developed Countries

Many people still dream that low-skill, high-wage manufacturing employment can and should be plentiful. But the reality is that in developed countries, the manufacturing economies of the 20th century are disappearing, replaced by higher-skill service jobs and creative jobs that warrant a higher wage because they are better suited for a global innovation economy (Florida, 2002). Manufacturing jobs still exist, but the pay and the work prospects are far bleaker than they used to be. The peak manufacturing employment in the United States was in June 1979 with 19.5 million manufacturing workers, but as of November 2016, that number was down to 12.3 million, or 37 percent fewer workers (Bureau of Labor Statistics, 2016). Similarly, the maximum wage available to the U.S. automobile factory workers that General Motors hired in 2015 was eight dollars fewer per hour (after adjusting for inflation) than for workers hired in 1961 (Ferla, 2011).

In Europe, similar patterns emerge. Fourteen of the sixteen countries economist David H. Autor (2014) studied saw increases in both low-wage occupations and high-wage occupations, with growth percentages generally higher for the higher-wage professions. However, all sixteen countries showed a tremendous loss of jobs with wages in the middle range. These trends are occurring in the economies of every developed country and even in some developing countries as well.

Manufacturers are more productive than ever, thanks to advances in technology and the advent of global supply chains. Yet despite that increased productivity, manufacturers generate fewer jobs for workers in their home countries. Every year the developed world loses manufacturing jobs to cheaper workers in developing countries, robots and other automation systems, and on-demand additive manufacturing (a process similar to 3-D printing at an industrial scale).

Additionally, the local manufacturing jobs that remain look much different from the traditional picture of workers on the factory line tightening bolts or assembling parts. *Advanced manufacturing* is the general term used for integration of technology systems and processes into manufacturing. The majority of manufacturing in developed countries will eventually be advanced manufacturing, and both advanced and additive manufacturing require workers with much more skill, training, education, and technological fluency than were ever expected of previous generations of factory workers. As a result, just as there is no foreseeable future in which printed text again dominates the media landscape, there also is no foreseeable future in which low-skill manufacturing dominates the advanced economies of the developed world.

If the middle sector of low-skill, high-wage manufacturing jobs that served as the gateway to the middle class for hundreds of millions of people are disappearing, what jobs are left? As of the writing of this book, the jobs that remain are primarily either low-skill, low-wage service jobs or high-skill, high-wage professional occupations (Autor & Price, 2013). Think home health-care aides and hotel room attendants—or software engineers and nanobiologists. In short, if workers today want high wages, they'd better have high skill levels to match. However, it's not just the low end of the high-wage job graph that's being squeezed.

Automation's Influence on High- and Low-Skill Jobs

Except for localized work that requires a human to be present on site (such as a barber or a surgeon), artificial intelligence, self-service economies, and other automation and labor substitution schemes are affecting high-skill jobs as well, promising to replace humans with software, robots, and less-expensive workers elsewhere (Brynjolfsson & McAfee, 2011; Levy & Murnane, 2004). It's increasingly the case that if part, most, or all of any job—including traditionally high-skill professional jobs—can be automated or otherwise turned into piecework, it will be, just as in manufacturing. For example, a company may make a multimillion-dollar investment in self-service tax preparation software to save money on tax preparers' salaries and benefits. Similarly, many high-level service jobs have at least a portion of work that can be outsourced more cheaply by using freelancers or independent contractors. In other words, it's not just cab drivers, telemarketers, secretaries, and retail salespeople who are in danger of losing their jobs. It's also architects, accountants, lawyers, and radiologists (Frey & Osborne, 2013).

What value do human workers in the developed world add that software, robots, or less-expensive workers from the developing world don't? It's imperative that we answer this question if we want to prevent our students from joining the ever-increasing pool of graduates who don't have the necessary skills to do higher-wage, irreplaceable professional work. As educators, we cannot continue to pretend that there are viable high-paying jobs for large numbers of low-skill graduates.

Our school systems now face pressure to upskill our workers so that they can engage in work beyond routine manual or cognitive labor. The challenge, however, is that our school systems were never designed to prepare large numbers of graduates to use what we've typically thought of as professional skills. Critical thinking, problem solving, creativity, and high-level communication and collaboration skills were previously reserved for the academic elite: the small sliver of our secondary students whom we prepared for college and professional careers. Our standardized schools were instead created to prepare mass numbers of citizens to engage in basic industrial work (or, later, basic office work)—in other words, for the exact jobs that are now declining in number at precipitous rates.

Today, higher-order-thinking skills are necessary not just for college but for nearly all citizenship and career demands (Wagner, 2008). Or, as Lauren B. Resnick (1987) of the U.S. National Research Council puts it:

> Although it is not new to include thinking, problem solving, and reasoning in *someone's* school curriculum, it is new to include it in *everyone's* curriculum. It is new to take seriously the aspiration of making thinking and problem solving a regular part of a school program for all of the population. . . . It is a new challenge to develop educational programs that assume that all individuals, not just an elite, can become competent thinkers. (p. 7)

Schools shouldn't just be about preparing corporate worker bees. In fact, we should be alarmed whenever we hear policymakers and others hint that the primary function of schools is to prepare graduates for certain careers or workforce needs. There are many other noble, important, and valuable missions for schools besides workforce development. But at the same time, schools can't ignore the global transformations that are reshaping careers and employment demands. As we think about our children and grandchildren, our nieces and nephews, our neighbors and our friends, we owe them employment and career options that at least have a fighting chance of being financially viable. To achieve this, we must make schools different.

Practical Steps and Strategies

- Pay more attention in instruction and assessment to nonautomatable 21st century skills such as critical thinking, problem solving, creativity, written and oral communication, teamwork and collaboration, leadership, and global awareness. For instance, at deeper learning school New Village Girls Academy (see chapter 7, page 43), students engage in projects and internships that regularly incorporate these skills.

- Conduct an internal cognitive complexity audit to determine what percentage of students' day-to-day work is factual recall and procedural regurgitation.

great idea!

- Initiate internal conversations, school board discussions, and community town halls about what it means to prepare future-ready students and graduates.

- Invite local and regional manufacturers and corporations to discuss with educators and parents the impacts of global competition and concurrent skill sets and hiring criteria in their work sector.

- Start implementing or deepening some of the ten building blocks described in the introduction (see page 5), along with the Future Ready Framework (Future Ready Schools, 2015), to begin reorienting toward the four big shifts that schools need to make.

- Encourage all staff to welcome the question, Why do we have to learn this? Consider the implications not only to career but also to citizenship.

Chapter 3
The Learning Argument

For most of human history, teachers and learning materials were extremely scarce. Because homes had few learning resources (such as books or maps) and often even fewer family members who were educated, any family that wanted to educate its young people had to rely on hiring individual tutors or on expensive travel to schools, universities, or libraries. As a result, formal learning was mostly reserved for the children of the elite and the wealthy, who had both the money and the time to educate them.

As time went on and teachers and learning materials became more widely available, factory-model schools began to emerge. The common schools movement occurred in America in the mid-1800s, and by the early 20th century, increasing numbers of students were persisting past the elementary grades and into secondary schools. These schools had the policy goal of educating the masses, and they broadened access to formal learning considerably. However, time and staffing were still scarcities, which resulted in organizing students by same-age groupings and grade-level curricula. These exigencies slotted learners into environments where, for the most part, they had to follow the same curriculum at the same pace as everyone else of their approximate age. In this chapter, we consider the evolution of instructional roles that is taking place in an era of abundant information access and the new teaching and learning opportunities technology affords us.

Evolution of Instructional Roles

We live in an era of information abundance rather than scarcity. Information that required travel to access is now available on our mobile phones, tablets, and laptops. This information also is no longer expensive: one of the marvels of our time is the sheer volume of learning materials that are easily accessible for free or at very low cost. Additionally, learning no longer has to occur during certain hours at a designated location; instead, it can take place "at any time, in any place, on any path, at any pace" (International Association for K–12 Online Learning, 2015). Many of the assumptions that gave rise to our current educational model no longer apply.

Take the subject of chemistry, for instance. As José Antonio Bowen (2012) notes, introductory topics in chemistry are "fairly predictable: atoms, orbitals, the mole, valence electrons, Lewis structures, and the periodic table" (p. 117). Bowen (2012) wonderfully describes the myriad ways that college or high school students could learn these topics without requiring face-to-face instruction or printed textbooks. For instance, there are well over a thousand chemistry tutorials, animations, lectures, instructional songs, and other videos on YouTube alone, some of which have been viewed hundreds of thousands of times. There are numerous mobile phone apps related to chemical formulas and the periodic table, including the Elements app that Apple featured when it launched the iPad. There is at least one online interactive periodic table and hundreds of chemistry-related Wikipedia articles. YouTube and iTunes U also offer thousands of chemistry-related video demonstrations. Additionally, there are chemistry podcasts, TED and TEDx lectures, and information from the National Science Digital Library, chemistry research journals, and the Khan Academy. Many chemistry professors make their course materials—including readings, tables, images and animations, interactive tutorials, and even complete textbooks—available to the public for free, and several university chemistry departments host deep, complex websites on various chemistry topics. Some of these sites even include experiments that can be done at home using consumer products, as well as randomly generated test questions that allow visitors to assess their understanding.

Full, free chemistry courses are available as well from top universities, including Carnegie Mellon, Yale, Massachusetts Institute of Technology, University of California at Berkeley, Tufts, and many others. These courses are typically offered through iTunes U, university-specific websites such as MIT OpenCourseWare and Open Yale, or other online course sites such as edX, Coursera, and Udemy. Internationally famous faculty, including Nobel Prize winners, teach many of these free courses, and they usually include syllabi, audio and video lectures, readings, lecture notes, exams and practice problems (with solutions), student study materials, and even resources for instructors and teaching assistants (Wilocis, 2016). Add in "websites that include chemistry quizzes, downloadable tests, and FAQs . . . online books at the Library of Congress . . . and plenty of wikibooks on chemistry" (Bowen, 2012, p. 120). Consider also chemistry websites that rank textbooks and other learning resources, and the joint chemistry portal from Multimedia Educational Resource for Learning and Online Teaching (MERLOT) and the *Journal of Chemical Education*. It is clear that the digital ecosphere for learning

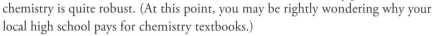

chemistry is quite robust. (At this point, you may be rightly wondering why your local high school pays for chemistry textbooks.)

This is just one subject, of course. The digital learning ecosystem for virtually every other academic subject is equally vigorous. But many K–12 educators have also left that ecosystem largely untapped, or at least not used it to the depth that Bowen (2012) describes. Most schools have yet to fully realize the implications of our new learning landscape. As Dean (Shareski, 2009) said long ago in a presentation slide, "School is no longer constrained to how far the bus can travel in the morning. Schools will be last to notice."

We believe we can safely say that students now don't need to come to school to learn the basics of chemistry. The Schlechty Center (2012) argues that the Internet is increasingly assuming the role of instructor, which has traditionally been the primary job of the teacher. While that statement may come as an affront to chemistry teachers, it simply suggests that if you're still teaching chemistry largely as a content-oriented learning experience—one in which the main focus is on memorizing facts and formulas—you are ripe for replacement.

If that's true, then what should a teacher's primary job be? Instead of being instructors themselves, teachers must shift their roles, becoming designers and guides to instruction. Because content is no longer scarce, our students don't need us to purvey information. But they do need us—now more than ever—to help them learn how to think about the content, wrestle and play with the content, and put the content to work. For many of our teachers and schools, this shift is extremely challenging and requires a drastically different approach to education. But if schools are to remain relevant societal institutions, acknowledging this challenge and acting upon it is essential.

Additionally important is the role teachers must learn to play in fostering interactions with other learners and organizations that purvey information. Our new learning landscape extends beyond the relatively passive use of digitized texts, audio, and video, or even beyond the use of interactive animations, simulations, and other multimedia. Learning increasingly includes interactions with others through connections that were impossible in the predigital world. Numerous foundations, advocacy groups, corporate associations, interest groups, and individuals other than academics create and share learning materials online, and many of the rich discussions they foster go well beyond information retrieval and regurgitation.

Technology Use

While this new connectivity seems to fall right in line with Abraham H. Maslow's (1943) ideas of student development and self-actualization, most schools tend to be extremely conservative in this area rather than embrace these opportunities. Schools supposedly have the universal mission of preparing students for lifelong learning and creating students ready to engage in modern careers. Yet most students still power down their devices when they come to school and only power up when they're using a computer at home or a mobile device in and around their communities (Prensky, 2008). As a result, learning at home, for students who have digital access, is often more powerful than learning at school.

Even when students do occasionally get access to the digital world while at school, that access typically occurs within very tightly constrained parameters. Unfortunately, tales abound of draconian filtering and blocking schemes within school systems. Our schools block Facebook, Twitter, Instagram, and other social media sites that they could use to foster student learning and connection to other classrooms and outside experts. Some schools block YouTube or Wikipedia. Others block Google. Still others block all blogs, as if there wasn't a single educationally worthy blog in existence.

Students aren't dumb. They know that many of the blocked sites are valuable, relevant, and meaningful in their lives outside of school. Therefore, an inevitable cat-and-mouse game occurs: students use inventive means (including filter bypasses and proxy servers) to try to access the world that surrounds them, while adults respond by continuing to wall off every new method of access.

Perhaps the most visibly egregious example of schools' lockdown mentality was the Los Angeles Unified School District's iPad fiasco (Moscaritolo, 2013). In 2013, students were handed iPads, which they could use for very little besides marching through the district-mandated curriculum via the district's highly restrictive custom-designed apps (that is, when those apps actually worked). When some of these students reasonably tried to change the settings of their allegedly personal devices so that they could engage in the same personal computing tasks the rest of us do—for example, listening to music, accessing the Internet, watching videos, or utilizing social media sites—both the district and the media labeled them hackers. The district was faced with a situation in which students actually had power over their own digital learning. One possibility for moving forward was to have a dialogue with those students, attempting to balance students' personal technology needs with the district's need to ensure that students met desired academic outcomes. Instead, the school district confiscated all the iPads (Moscaritolo, 2013). So much for its much-ballyhooed $1.3 billion technology initiative.

As Audrey Watters (2013) noted at the time, Los Angeles Unified had "a profound lack of vision about how students themselves could use—want to use—these new technologies to live and to learn at their fullest potential." But that "profound lack of vision" permeates schools' use of instructional technologies. We not only see schools purchasing digital learning tools and then trying desperately to prevent students from using them but also showing little understanding of the changes in instruction and policy that are necessary to fully prepare graduates to be empowered, technology-using citizens.

In a digital world, those who know how to interact, share, and collaborate online have a greater likelihood of success than those who don't. There are specific skills required to have a positive digital presence: students should know how to utilize blogs, social media, Creative Commons licenses, and other mechanisms to share their knowledge and skills, as well as how to find and participate in online learning communities as both consumers and contributors. Yet few schools teach these skills. Instead, they craft acceptable use policies that lecture students about all the things that they can't do and all the ways that they can get in trouble if they dare to be noncompliant.

Because of these fearful, finger-wagging messages that we send students about using technology, the impacts of digital learning tools are sparse at best. Aside from a few brave, isolated classroom innovators who take advantage of the new affordances that digital tools bring, most student and teacher technology use is a more expensive replication of what was previously done in analog environments. Think interactive whiteboards instead of chalkboards and YouTube videos instead of filmstrips.

The National Council of Teachers of English (NCTE) has weighed in on what it means to be literate these days. Its updated 21st Century Literacies Framework (NCTE, 2013) recognizes the seismic impacts of our new information landscape on what it means today to be a reader, a writer, a digital information consumer, and a multimedia producer. Literacies such as the ability to "design and share information for global communities that have a variety of purposes" or to "manage, analyze, and synthesize multiple streams of simultaneously presented information" or to "create, critique, analyze, and evaluate multimedia texts" often look like slightly different lenses on old conceptions of literacy, although their actual implementation often requires vastly different skill sets and proficiencies (NCTE, 2013, p. 1). Researchers such as Henry Jenkins (2006), Mizuko Ito and colleagues (2010), danah boyd (2014), and Colin Lankshear and Michele Knobel (2011) echo and elaborate on these new literacies.

But what's striking and dismaying about these new literacies is how few English and language arts teachers even know about them, are implementing them, or would be considered literate themselves under their own professional association's new framework. As a result, we continue to turn out students who are illiterate within our current information landscape, left to fend for themselves after graduation within an incredibly complex, global, technology-suffused information commons.

If students and graduates are to become true masters of that world, they must begin to realize the profound possibilities that result from sharing and interconnectedness. Our students must be taught to be adaptive, self-directed, empowered learners able to reorient and upskill themselves as needed to meet rapidly changing economic and workforce demands. They must learn how to be online and media

Something many educators struggle with I think!

Who will teach them ?!

literate, not just text literate. They must learn how to be content creators, not just content consumers. And they must learn how to use our powerful digital learning and productivity tools in ways that allow them to add value above and beyond what machines alone can do. Real, tangible value inheres when we help students become connected to online sharing communities.

When we instead hold students back due to our own fears, lack of knowledge, or unwillingness to give up control, we deliberately hamstring their chances of success. Students don't learn the skills they need in traditional learning spaces that aggressively filter out the Internet or that orient them toward passive listening to oral lectures and compliant recall and regurgitation from texts—even if those lectures and texts happen to be delivered digitally. Yet these are the spaces students are subjected to almost every single school day. We are wasting a lot of student potential because we refuse or can't figure out how to make schools different.

Practical Steps and Strategies

- Use NCTE's (2013) 21st Century Literacies Framework to facilitate internal and community conversations about modern-day multiliteracies (O'Rourke, 2005) versus traditional print literacy.

- Re-examine acceptable use policies, Internet filters, administrative messaging, and other system-level signals that may impede empowered student and educator technology use.

- Actively seek opportunities for students to be local and digital content creators and sharers (not just consumers) and to create positive community and digital footprints. The students at the deeper learning school Ao Tawhiti Unlimited Discovery (see chapter 7, page 46), do this in nearly all of their community-embedded projects.

- Be intentional about creating structured avenues for students to participate in online communities of learning.

- Utilize the trudacot (technology-rich unit design and classroom observation template) discussion protocol (McLeod, n.d.; bit.ly /trudacot) to help foster robust technology infusion and realign lesson plans and instructional units toward deeper learning, greater student agency, and authentic work.

- Value learning that takes place outside school. For elementary students in particular, think about homework that honors all the learning that takes place at home and in the community.

Chapter 4
The Boredom Argument

We've known for a long time that many, many students are bored in school. We see the signs in classrooms everywhere. Students slump down, eyelids heavy, or they slouch over with their heads on their desks. They gaze out the window, hoping for something more interesting than what's occurring in front of them. They doodle and pass notes and try to sneak a peek at Facebook. Anything to relieve the tedium. In this chapter, we look at the influence of teaching materials and assignments on student engagement and examine how cognitive demand affects this engagement.

Influence of Teaching Materials and Assignments

The daily rhythms of many classrooms are driven by educational publishing companies' materials, which have been sanitized, edited, and censored to remove any content that might be potentially controversial and, thus, interesting (Ravitch, 2003). Students sit and listen or read for hour after hour, class period after class period, while their teachers or textbooks (or now, YouTube videos) drone on about topics that are of little interest. At the end of each lesson, they answer review questions or do practice problems that have little relevance to their daily lives, or maybe teachers hand them a worksheet or quiz that's intended to assess their knowledge and understanding but that fails to concern itself with whether they will actually care about the topic for any longer than the teacher forces them to. More often than not, chapter review questions, practice problems, worksheets, and quizzes focus on low-level items of factual recall and procedural regurgitation, exactly the types of information that students can find with a two-second online search with Google or Siri.

Even when students get to do a "project," it typically consists of the presentation of low-level facts in some colorful but still regurgitative format. We've all seen these: sugar cube pyramids, Styrofoam ball solar systems, coat hanger mobiles, cereal box book reports, and dioramas. Or maybe our students make posters, paper brochures, or PowerPoint presentations. Or they make structures out of construction paper, wire, cardboard, tape, or papier-mâché. John Dewey (1916) reminded us over a century ago that we learn what we do, yet most of the doing in projects like these involves creating the physical structure of the model rather than engaging with the academic content.

If you ask students to describe school in a word and tabulate the most common results, it's more likely than not that the word *boring* will be near the top of the list. This is nothing new: our students have checked out from school both mentally and physically for decades on end. But we've always tended to focus on those who physically disengage—tardies, absences, and dropouts—and much less on those who drop out mentally. As long as students are physically present and compliant, school systems are happy, and so are we as educators.

Influence of Cognitive Demand on Engagement

As a result, our responses to student disengagement are often both sparse and unsatisfying, and they have been for well over a century. Don't believe us? Believe Dewey (1916), who says in *Democracy and Education* that:

> The chief source of the "problem of discipline" in schools is that . . . a premium is put on physical quietude; on silence, on rigid uniformity of posture and movement; upon a machine-like simulation of the attitudes of intelligent interest. The teachers' business is to hold the pupils up to these requirements and to punish the inevitable deviations which occur. (p. 165)

Half a century later, Neil Postman and Charles Weingartner (1969) say:

> Now, what is it that students do in the classroom? Well, mostly, they sit and listen to the teacher. . . . Mostly, they are required to remember. . . . It is practically unheard of for students to play any role in determining what problems are worth studying or what procedures of inquiry ought to be used. (p. 19)

By 1984, a year after *A Nation at Risk*, John I. Goodlad notes in his landmark book, *A Place Called School*, that:

> The data from our observations in more than 1,000 classrooms support the popular image of a teacher standing or sitting in front of a class imparting knowledge to a group of students. Explaining and lecturing constituted the most frequent teaching activities. . . . And the frequency of these activities increased steadily from the primary to the senior high school years. Teachers also spent a substantial amount of time observing students at work or monitoring their seatwork. . . . Our data show not only an increase in these activities but also a decline in teachers interacting with groups of students within their classes from the primary to the secondary years. . . . Three cat-

egories of student activity marked by passivity—written work, listening, and preparing for assignments—dominate. . . . The chances are
better than 50–50 that if you were to walk into any of the classrooms
of our sample, you would see one of these three activities under way.
. . . All three activities are almost exclusively set and monitored by
teachers. We saw a contrastingly low incidence of activities invoking
active modes of learning. (p. 105)

Two decades later, Mike Schmoker (2006) cites a study of more than fifteen hundred classroom observations to make the following claims.

- **Classrooms in which there was evidence of higher-order thinking:**
  3 percent

- **Classrooms in which teachers used high-yield instructional
  strategies:** 0.2 percent

- **Classrooms in which fewer than one-half of students were paying
  attention:** 85 percent

Also in 2006, Richard F. Elmore, who holds an endowed professorship at Harvard
University, notes that "when [we] code classroom practice for level of cognitive
demand . . . 80 percent of the work is at the factual and procedural level" and that
"[teachers] will do low-level work and call it high-level work." In 2007, Robert
C. Pianta, later the dean of the Curry School of Education at the University of
Virginia, and his co-authors report in a study of over twenty-five hundered classrooms in more than one thousand elementary schools across four hundred school
districts that "the average fifth grader received five times as much instruction in
basic skills as instruction focused on problem solving or reasoning; this ratio was
10:1 in first and third grades" (Pianta, Belsky, Houts, & Morrison, p. 2).

Study after study, anecdote after anecdote, decade after decade all confirm that
the work we typically ask students to do is dull, trivial, and thoroughly uninspiring.
This is what's known as a structural problem. It's not the fault of a small handful
of boring teachers or of a few students who simply don't fit in. This is millions of
students, year after year, who are bored out of their minds as we ask them to play
"the game of school" (Fried, 2005): a game in which success consists primarily of
regurgitating low-level information that students could care less about. Student disengagement is an egregiously ignored and ongoing challenge, one that few schools
have been willing to face head-on.

A 2016 Gallup poll surveyed American students about their engagement in
schools. The results are sobering. In elementary school, 75 percent of students said
that they were engaged in what they were learning. By eighth grade, however, that
already-low figure had decreased to 45 percent, and by the end of high school it
was 34 percent. To get these figures, Gallup asked some very specific questions. The
responses to these revealed that only one-third of high school students said that

they'd learned something interesting at school in the past week, only 20 percent said that they had fun at school, and less than 20 percent said that, at their school, they got to do what they do best every day (Gallup, 2016).

A tightly controlled environment in which you're not having fun, don't get to do what you do best, and aren't learning anything interesting isn't exactly a recipe for motivation and engagement. Yet that's the reality that most students face day in and day out, class after class, year after year. The biggest indictment we can make about our schools is not their failure to raise test scores above some politically determined line of "proficiency"; it's that they routinely ignore the fact that students are bored, disengaged, and disempowered. We've known this forever, but we have yet to really care about it in a way that would drive substantive changes in practice. As a result, our youth continue to be disenfranchised by the very institutions that are supposed to prepare them to be lifelong learners.

Here's a challenge for you: add up all the students in your local secondary school who have physically checked out—in other words, they've dropped out or have chronic attendance problems. Then add to that number all the students who have mentally checked out—in other words, they're at school because their friends are there and the law requires it, but they're not really engaged in their learning. They're just biding time, hoping that whatever comes next in their lives is more interesting. In most secondary schools, this overall total will easily make up half of the student body, and sometimes two-thirds or more (Gallup, 2016; Kamenetz, 2016).

George Couros (2014) asks teachers a very pointed question in regard to boredom and engagement: "Would you want to be a learner in your own classroom?" We can—and should—do better for our students, but we do that by making schools different.

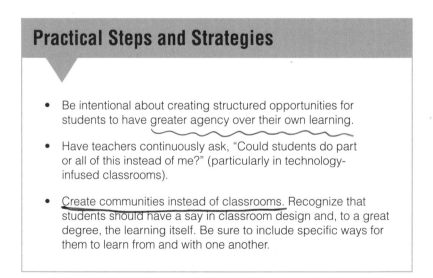

Practical Steps and Strategies

- Be intentional about creating structured opportunities for students to have greater agency over their own learning.

- Have teachers continuously ask, "Could students do part or all of this instead of me?" (particularly in technology-infused classrooms).

- Create communities instead of classrooms. Recognize that students should have a say in classroom design and, to a great degree, the learning itself. Be sure to include specific ways for them to learn from and with one another.

- Utilize an observation protocol or assessment such as the Instructional Practices Inventory (Valentine, 2005) to assess student engagement with their learning activities.

- Explore inquiry- and project-based learning methods—and service learning within local and online communities—that would allow students to engage in more meaningful, authentic, real-world work. Deeper learning school Iowa BIG (see chapter 7, page 42), does an excellent job of this through its community project pool.

- Implement various organizational and instructional structures—including adaptive learning software systems and blended learning models—that further personalization and differentiation of student learning.

Done well and done by ALL!

Chapter 5
The Innovation Argument

Schools usually are nice places. The people who work in them are friendly, and most of them care about kids and are trying to do right by the students and families that they serve. What's more, they're often doing this despite being underfunded, under-resourced, and underappreciated. In other words, they are making genuine and sincere attempts to prepare our youth for their futures.

Despite this goodwill, it's hard to think of environments in which timely innovation takes more of a back seat than in schools. The old joke is that if Rip Van Winkle fell asleep one hundred years ago and woke up today, he would be bewildered by all of the changes that have occurred. But then he'd walk into a classroom and feel instantly at home.

As noted in chapter 4 (page 21), much of the lack of innovation among students has to do with schools' overwhelming emphasis on compliance. Teachers and administrators' relentless efforts to control young people in every aspect of their school lives exact a terrible toll on students' willingness to think outside the box. When hundreds of millions of students get told exactly what to do every minute of every school day for thirteen years—and when they're punished for noncompliance—we should not be surprised that few are willing to take risks, try new things, or think in uncharted directions. The seventeen-year-old boy who is still required to raise his hand and ask to go to the bathroom isn't going to push the limits of his learning environment. The eight-year-old girl who has already internalized that there is one right answer isn't going to spend much time searching for divergent processes or solutions. Just as it's difficult to prepare high-level thinkers in low-level know-ledge environments, it's also a challenge to prepare innovators in compliance-heavy learning spaces. In this chapter, we'll examine key skills necessary for innovation, the types of environments that foster innovation, and the need for teachers to have choice and flexibility in their instruction in order to develop innovative thinkers.

Key Skills for Innovation

Beyond boredom and disengagement, what other factors prevent schools from producing innovators? Jeffrey H. Dyer, Hal Gregersen, and Clayton M. Christensen (2009) note there are five key skills of innovators: (1) associating, (2) questioning, (3) observing, (4) experimenting, and (5) networking. To answer our question, let's look at each in turn.

Associating is "the ability to successfully connect seemingly unrelated questions, problems, or ideas from different fields" (Dyer et al., 2009). Steve Jobs, former CEO of Apple, said repeatedly throughout his career that "creativity is connecting things" (Wolf, 1996). But in school, students rarely get a chance to connect content and ideas in interesting and interdisciplinary ways. When schools segregate subject areas into disconnected forty-five-minute blocks of time, students' ability to associate across different academic areas is at best an anomaly or wishful thinking. Add to this unfortunate situation the fact that teachers themselves struggle with associating across different academic areas. What can a mathematics teacher and a language arts teacher learn from one another? What can a kindergarten teacher and a high school biology teacher learn from one another? Many teachers and administrators would see no value in such superficially disparate pairings.

The second key skill of innovators is *questioning*. Innovators ask questions like "Why?" and "Why not?" and "What if?" (Dyer et al., 2009). The importance of questioning has long been recognized. For instance, Postman and Weingartner (1969) say, "Once you have learned how to ask questions—relevant and appropriate and substantial questions—you have learned how to learn and no one can keep you from learning whatever you want or need to know" (p. 23). Dan Rothstein and Luz Santana (2011) reiterate that teaching students to ask their own questions can be a powerful catalyst for deeper learning. The art of asking good questions seemingly falls right in line with schools' stated missions of preparing lifelong learners. But as Postman and Weingartner (1969) note, in most classrooms:

> What students are restricted to (solely and even vengefully) is the process of memorizing . . . somebody else's answers to somebody else's questions. It is staggering to consider the implications of this fact. The most important intellectual ability man has yet developed—the art and science of asking questions—is not taught in school! Moreover, it is not "taught" in the most devastating way possible: by arranging the environment so that significant question asking is not valued. It is doubtful if you can think of many schools that include question asking, or methods of inquiry, as part of their curriculum. (pp. 23–24)

Nearly half a century later, these observations still ring true. Even when teachers occasionally encourage students to ask questions about what they're studying, many students are so disengaged—due to dull content, uninteresting learning tasks, and the overwhelming institutional emphasis on convergent rather than divergent thinking—that they wonder why they should even bother. We have overvalued the importance of students giving answers and undervalued the potential of students asking questions.

The third and fourth skills of innovators are *observing* and *experimenting*. In other words, innovators scrutinize everyday phenomena with the goal of uncovering new ideas and solutions. Innovators are social scientists, trying to investigate patterns and gaps in the everyday in order to uncover meaning.

Yet in most schools, teachers spoon-feed students whatever information they want students to learn, and opportunities for genuine inquiry are rare. As Tony Wagner (2008) notes, even science "experiments" tend to be more like recipes than true explorations: students blindly follow the steps that the teacher or the lab manual gives them rather than engaging in authentic investigations where the outcome is unknown. If the experiment achieves "correct" results, students dutifully write down their "findings" in the format the teacher prescribes. If the experiment fails to achieve the desired results, students have no idea why: the conceptual understanding that genuine inquiry would have generated is not there. The number of opportunities for students to truly experiment in most schools is virtually nil.

Schools function through set curricula with set learning standards and set outcomes. The school assesses those outcomes with one-size-fits-all grading and testing instruments designed to move everyone toward one set of correct responses. The job of students is not to deviate but to regurgitate. Due to content coverage pressures and teacher control needs, any divergence from the established path is off-task by definition.

What we need is much more divergence from the established path. Douglas Thomas and John Seely Brown (2011) suggest that play may be the most important element in creating new learning environments. While play has traditionally been relegated to young children and viewed as something that we grow out of as we mature and learn, in a world of constant change we must embrace play and experimentation as key ingredients in continual learning. Play seems anti-intellectual for many people but in fact, it is quite the opposite. As Neville V. Scarfe (1962) stated decades ago, "The highest form of research is essentially play" (p. 120).

The fifth and final key skill of innovators is *networking*. Innovators expose themselves to a variety of people and perspectives, pulling together ideas and practices in ways that add value to their own domain. But although networking is vital in the real world outside of the classroom walls, students in schools remain isolated, with few opportunities to interact in substantive ways either with each other or with people outside of the classroom. There are occasional guest speakers or webcam experts, but those visits are rarely an open, freewheeling exchange of ideas that add value for both parties; instead, the visitor typically talks at the students while they sit and listen passively. Few schools help students create and nurture active networks of other students and outside adult individuals and organizations that would drive their learning forward.

Environments That Foster Innovation

Tony Wagner has spent much of his career studying environments that nurture innovation. He has interviewed young artists, scientists, and engineers; talked to entrepreneurs and founders of start-up companies; and had discussions with leaders of some of the most innovative companies and organizations in the world. Building on the work of Teresa M. Amabile (1998), Wagner (2012a) notes that expertise, creative-thinking skills, and motivation all work together to foster innovation. These qualities are fostered by environments that exhibit strong cultures of teamwork, interdisciplinary problem solving, and intrinsic incentives such as exploration, play, and empowerment.

Read those previous two sentences again. *Creative thinking, interdisciplinary problem solving, empowerment*, and *motivation*: Do these describe the classrooms in your schools? For most students, the answer is an emphatic *no*, usually because classrooms are focused on convergent compliance rather than on divergent or collaborative creativity. To illustrate this point, Wagner (2012b) surveyed dozens of young adults whom he deemed to be innovators in some respect. He asked the young adults to identify a teacher who had a significant influence on their current career. Most couldn't name one, and those who did referenced teachers who had a reputation as outsiders or noncompliers.

As Wagner (2012a) notes:

> The way in which academic content is taught is often stultifying: It is too often merely a process of transferring information through rote memorization, with few opportunities for students to ask questions or discover things on their own—the essential practices of innovation. (p. 141)

This is sharply at odds with the needs of our society. We've always needed innovators to some extent, but globalization has created a significantly greater imperative for schools to graduate them.

During the period when transportation and communication limitations kept most interactions local, it was relatively easy to be the only one within a certain geographic area who could provide a particular product or service. In a globalized world, however, people and organizations across the planet compete with us at equivalent service levels and often at lower prices. Countless others make competing products and services available with a tap on a smartphone or the click of a mouse. If we want to stay ahead of these competitors, innovation is a constant requirement. We must improve our offerings just to survive.

We also have seen a dramatic rise in the freelancing economy. Competitive economic pressures have driven corporations, universities, nonprofits, government agencies, and other employers to reduce their investments in full-time employees and instead rely on independent contractors and freelancers, creating a so-called *gig economy*. As many as a third of American workers, for instance, may now be engaged in freelance work, with at least part of their income dependent on a succession of independently negotiated work gigs (Horowitz, 2015). Dennis Yang (2016) notes:

> These independent workers need to keep hustling to stay ahead of the curve and prove they can out-innovate their peers. In short, as more companies choose to depend on contract workers for key parts of their business, those freelancers will see increasing competition for those gigs and, therefore, more pressure to differentiate themselves and their skills.

Are most schools teaching students to leverage their individual interests and skill sets to out-innovate their peers and differentiate themselves from the crowd? Are most schools teaching students to adopt entrepreneurial mindsets, workflows, and financing techniques in order to be both self-sufficient and competitive in a highly complex and rapidly shifting work landscape? Are most schools teaching students to upskill themselves so that they optimize their chances to be selected for the next gig that they're seeking? Nope.

Instead, do most schools still primarily run students through a one-size-fits-all model, assess students in standardized ways, discount students' unique strengths and talents, and ignore the economic and workplace realities into which they'll send their supposedly qualified graduates? Do most schools still pretend that regurgitation of the same boring stuff that everyone else also sat through is adequate preparation for an innovation society? Yep.

Innovation is how we initiate movement beyond the status quo. Innovation is how we transform school structures and educator mindsets from the world as it was to the world as it is and will be. Innovation is *important*. But most schools don't have an innovation agenda. Instead, we make a few tweaks here and there, or we institute a new program that benefits a small number of students without significantly impacting the vast majority. And we pat ourselves on the back for doing something, anything, even if its transformative impact is minimal and marginal.

Innovation can't be fostered through simplistic approaches. It requires a transformation of mindset and culture, not just a script or a scope and sequence plan. But such a transformation represents an immediate challenge to the culture of compliance and conformity in schools. Innovation and "best practices" can (and do) butt heads. Innovation often means that we won't or can't know the outcome of our attempts in advance. That ambiguity is not something that many schools are prepared to address.

But we need to address it. Technology companies describe the organic process of focusing on rapid, iterative change with frequent feedback loops as _living in perpetual beta_. Schools must do a much better job—on numerous fronts—of living in perpetual beta. Otherwise their pace of change is doomed to remain glacial, and their relevance gap with the society around them will continue to widen. As John Merrow (2012) asks so adroitly, "Who is going to hire young people skilled at regurgitation?" To keep that gap from widening, we must make schools different.

Teachers' Lack of Choice and Flexibility

Here's one final note on this topic. Most of our frontline classroom educators operate within the same innovation-challenged environments as our students. Administrators tell them what to do, just as compliance-focused teachers tell students. And if those frontline educators deviate from generally accepted norms of behavior or practice, those administrators may punish them formally, or their peers may do so informally.

Most school systems mandate the content and form of teachers' professional learning, and they rarely give teachers meaningful input or choice regarding instructional standards, curricula, textbooks and other learning materials, daily schedules, learning outcomes, or other aspects of their professional work. Some schools even mandate that teachers use scripted lessons, questions, and responses, essentially removing all discretion from their classroom roles. While administrators and policymakers often command, dictate, and direct the individuals whom they expect to carry out their innovation agendas, it's much rarer that they listen to, empower, or self-actualize these educators.

The level of meaningful voice and choice for classroom educators is fairly low in many school buildings, and when a few isolated teachers are brave enough to take a risk, they open themselves up to criticism and envy from many of their peers. This creates what's known as a _crab bucket culture_ (Margolis, 2014), also known as _tall poppy syndrome_ (Mouly & Sankaran, 2002), where groups in a system try to undermine any individual's attempt to be successful or break free of that system's constraints. Such cultures are alive and dangerous in many schools.

This state of affairs—authoritarian administrators and disparaging peers— creates tightly controlled, fearful teachers who take few instructional risks. If we want teachers to enable student agency and inquiry, we must enable agency and inquiry for them as well.

Most of the burden of changing this culture falls on the shoulders of administrators and policymakers. Policymakers must pay more attention to the kinds of workplace demands that future graduates will face, and school administrators must build cultures of innovation by giving up some of their decision-making authority— as well as developing some trust in their teachers.

The fact that we have such difficulty recognizing and acting on this basic fact shows how deeply embedded the culture of compliance is within our schools. Unfortunately, our factory-model schools will continue to disengage both students and teachers until we make schools different. What's more, they'll continue to deny students the chance to gain critical innovative capacities relevant to the world around them.

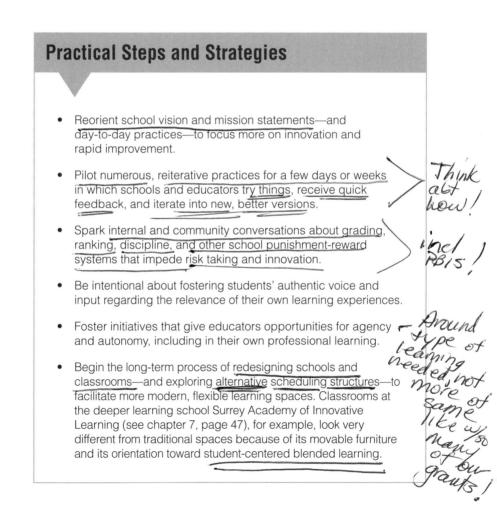

Practical Steps and Strategies

- Reorient school vision and mission statements—and day-to-day practices—to focus more on innovation and rapid improvement.

- Pilot numerous, reiterative practices for a few days or weeks in which schools and educators try things, receive quick feedback, and iterate into new, better versions. *[handwritten: Think abt how!]*

- Spark internal and community conversations about grading, ranking, discipline, and other school punishment-reward systems that impede risk taking and innovation. *[handwritten: incl PBIS!]*

- Be intentional about fostering students' authentic voice and input regarding the relevance of their own learning experiences.

- Foster initiatives that give educators opportunities for agency and autonomy, including in their own professional learning. *[handwritten: Around type of learning needed, not more of same]*

- Begin the long-term process of redesigning schools and classrooms—and exploring alternative scheduling structures—to facilitate more modern, flexible learning spaces. Classrooms at the deeper learning school Surrey Academy of Innovative Learning (see chapter 7, page 47), for example, look very different from traditional spaces because of its movable furniture and its orientation toward student-centered blended learning. *[handwritten: like w/ so many of our grants!]*

Chapter 6
The Equity Argument

Even if schools made changes in all of the preceding areas, concerns would still exist if they left out certain student populations. And even when schools do move toward creating more modern learning environments, the evidence indicates that such moves continue age-old inequities among students—and in some cases even exacerbate them. In this chapter, we'll reflect on the academic achievement and technology usage discrepancies among demographics in student populations and the discrepancies in the types of technology usage opportunities these students encounter in school.

Demographic Discrepancies in Academic Achievement and Technology Usage

Achievement gaps have long existed within measures of student learning. Traditionally disadvantaged student populations—students of color, students in poverty, students who have disabilities or who are non-native English speakers—generally do worse on the SAT, ACT, NAEP, and other American national- and state-level standardized assessments, regardless of grade level or subject area. American students exhibit similar gaps on large-scale international assessments such as PISA, Trends in International Mathematics and Science Study (TIMSS), and Progress in International Reading Literacy Study (PIRLS). Quite sizable discrepancies also continue in grade point averages, behavioral punishments at school, suspension and expulsion rates, high school graduation rates, and college attendance and persistence rates. Despite decades of attention, billions of dollars, and countless policy initiatives intended to close these gaps, we continue to underserve large sections of our student population.

The disadvantaging of certain student subpopulations manifests itself in numerous ways within our school buildings and classrooms. We direct many underserved, underachieving students to double down on basic academic content in the hope of getting them over the proficiency line on some standardized achievement test. The dominant belief is that these students just need longer and more intense doses of the same type of education rather than something different. Meanwhile their more-advantaged and higher-achieving student peers have greater access to in-school and extracurricular learning opportunities that are more likely to foster college and career readiness.

Unsurprisingly, these persistent educational inequities extend to students' use of digital tools and online environments as well. Since the 1980s, the question of access has been one of the dominant conversations in educational technology. Many schools struggle to provide basic computer and Internet access to students because of philosophical, financial, or pedagogical challenges. As a result, students and families in poverty—including, sometimes, those of color—experience reduced rates of access to desktop, tablet, and mobile computers, and they are less likely to have high-speed home access to the Internet (or even access to the Internet at all). Although progress has been made on this digital divide in many communities, there are still areas—particularly in urban and rural regions—where significant numbers of families and children don't have access to the basic tools necessary for success in a technology-infused world.

A report from the Joan Ganz Cooney Center (Rideout & Katz, 2016) underscores the scale of this problem in the United States. As the authors note:

> Most low- and moderate-income families have some form of Internet connection, but many are under-connected, with mobile-only access and inconsistent connectivity. Nine in ten (94%) families have some kind of Internet access, whether through a computer and Internet connection at home, or through a smart mobile device with a data plan. Even among families below the poverty level, nine in ten (91%) are connected in some way. However, many lower-income families are under-connected. For example, one quarter (23%) of families below the median income level and one third (33%) of those below the poverty level rely on mobile-only Internet access. And many experience interruptions to their Internet service or constrained access to digital devices. Among families who have home Internet access, half (52%) say their access is too slow, one quarter (26%) say too many people share the same computer, and one fifth (20%) say their Internet has been cut off in the last year due to lack of payment. Among families with mobile-only access, three in ten (29%) say they have hit the data limits on their plan in the past year, one-quarter (24%) say they have had their phone service cut off in the past year due to lack of payment, and one fifth (21%) say too many people share the same phone for them to be able to get the time on it that they need. (p. 5)

Moreover, the report also notes that although most low-income families cite cost as the primary barrier, a mere 6 percent say that they have ever signed up for low-cost access through programs created specifically for lower-income families (Rideout & Katz, 2016).

Discrepancies in Ways Students Utilize Technology in School

Lack of access translates to lower usage. Students from families with limited access to computing devices and the Internet are thus less able to go online to access school materials, engage in digital learning opportunities, pursue their interests and passions, or make contributions to online communities. In short, technology further extends the advantages that many of their school peers already possess. As a result, the achievement gap widens further.

Unfortunately, access is not the only barrier underserved students face when it comes to learning technologies: even when these students do get to use technology at school, they frequently use it in very limited ways compared to their more affluent and higher-achieving classmates. To illustrate this issue, let's take a look at two U.S. studies.

Harold Wenglinsky's (1998) study examines the population of American eighth graders who took the 1996 NAEP mathematics exam. Of that population, 34 percent said that they used computers primarily for drill and practice, while only 27 percent said that they used computers for higher-level simulations or applications. That result isn't surprising, given American schools' emphasis on lower-level factual recall and procedural regurgitation. But Wenglinsky (1998) also found an enormous usage divide along racial lines: while only 30 percent of white students said that they used computers primarily for drill and practice, a whopping 52 percent of African American students did so. The usage divide along socioeconomic status was smaller—34 percent of students on free and reduced-price lunch said that they used computers primarily for drill and practice compared to only 31 percent of the more affluent students—but still present.

Fast forward fifteen years to 2011, well after policymakers and administrators across the United States had begun to implement accountability movements to decrease academic achievement gaps and initiatives to increase students' digital access. Despite these efforts, another study of American eighth graders taking the NAEP mathematics exam (Rich, 2013) showed that the numbers had gotten worse. While the same 34 percent of students overall said that they used computers primarily for drill and practice, now "less than a quarter worked with spreadsheets or geometric figures on the computer. Only 17 percent used statistical programs" (Rich, 2013, p. A17). The large racial disparities in computer usage were essentially unchanged since 1996 and, sadly, the socioeconomic usage gap had increased from 3 to 11 percentage points during this time; more than 40 percent of the students eligible for free and reduced lunch said that they were using computers primarily for drill and practice compared to only 29 percent of their more affluent peers (Boser, 2013). As Justin Reich (2013) dismayingly summarizes: "Fifteen years apart. Different computers. Maybe different software. . . . Same patterns of usage. Persistent inequality."

These types of discrepancies in technology usage—sometimes referred to as the *secondary digital divide*—exist in most of our schools. Certain groups of students get to use technology in creative and empowering ways, while others primarily react to practice exercises that the computer inflicts on them. Our failure to make progress on this front is embarrassing.

In our technology-suffused world, both digital divides—access and usage—are of equally grave concern. Students who get to use digital technologies in robust ways that foster their learning and community involvement have a much greater chance at success in life than those who don't get this opportunity. Because of this, schools and communities must pay more than lip service to issues of digital equity. Few schools have done any sort of digital equity audit to assess students' level of basic access at school and home, as well as to uncover the ways in which schools allow students to make use of digital technologies. Until schools take digital equity seriously, they will continue to exacerbate the gaps between the haves and the have-nots, and they will continue to deny our most disadvantaged students opportunities for relevant education. Students who have access to digital tools and content are lucky, but you shouldn't have to be lucky to learn. As we work to make schools different, we must pay attention to equity.

Practical Steps and Strategies

- Recognize that ensuring access to higher-level instructional experiences and deeper learning opportunities is as important as addressing achievement gaps on lower-level standardized tests. Many deeper learning schools—including New Village Girls Academy (see chapter 7, page 43)—are explicitly designed around the idea that higher-level thinking work can lead to significant improvements on traditional assessments.

- Survey families to get a clear picture of students' home access to technology and the Internet, and discuss the school system's possible assistance (community partnerships, Wi-Fi buses, neighborhood Internet kiosks, serving as an Internet service provider, and so on) for underserved neighborhoods and communities.

- Conduct instructional and digital equity audits to determine which students have access to robust learning and technology opportunities in schools and which do not.

- Spark internal and community conversations about instructional and technology equity and their relationship to the future readiness and life success of graduates.

- Utilize the International Society for Technology in Education's Essential Conditions (2017a) and the Lead and Transform Diagnostic Tool (2017b) to inform technology access initiatives and integration planning.

Chapter 7
The Alternative

Fortunately, not all is doom and gloom: numerous deeper learning schools have already embarked on the transformational journey we advocate. Although they by no means represent even a significant minority at the time of this writing, there are hundreds and possibly even thousands of schools worldwide that show us what might be possible.

Research has proven repeatedly that deeper learning environments work. Comprehensive studies on students and graduates of deeper learning schools, which the Hewlett Foundation commissioned and the American Institutes for Research published, find that students in school environments that focus on deeper thinking, student inquiry, and project-based learning generally outperform traditional public school students on international assessments of reading, mathematics, and science core content, critical thinking, and complex problem-solving skills (Zeiser, Taylor, Rickles, Garet, & Segeritz, 2014). These students also outperform student peers on more traditional state tests in mathematics and English or language arts, and they report greater collaboration skills and exhibit higher levels of academic engagement, motivation to learn, and self-efficacy. They also are more likely to graduate on time and are more likely to enroll in four-year colleges and universities (Zeiser, Mills, Wulach, & Garet, 2016; Zeiser et al., 2014). These latter results are particularly true for students who enter high school with low achievement, which indicates that deeper learning schools are more effective at getting lower-achieving youth back on track.

Other research within individual deeper learning networks in the United States echoes these findings. For instance, when it comes to higher-order-thinking skills, New Tech Network (2015) students have 65 percent greater growth than national comparison groups between freshman and senior years of high school. They graduate from high school at a rate 14 percent higher than the national average, and they enroll in college at a rate that is 6 percent higher. Their college persistence rate is an extraordinary 92 percent at four-year colleges and 74 percent at two-year institutions (New Tech Network, 2015). Similarly, after only three years, students in Expeditionary Learning (EL) Education middle schools experience positive learning impacts equal to an extra seven months of growth in reading and ten extra months of growth in mathematics (EL Education, 2016). Students in the EdVisions Schools (2009) have higher levels of autonomy, belongingness, academic press, and mastery goal orientation, as well as higher rates of college enrollment. Nearly 86 percent of High Tech High alumni are still in or have graduated from college, compared to a national rate of 59 percent, and 35 percent of those graduates are first-generation college students. Over 30 percent of High Tech High alumni enter mathematics or science fields, compared to a national rate of 17 percent (High Tech High, 2015). Across the board, deeper learning schools are achieving the results that we say we want for our students.

In the pages that follow, we profile a few schools that we think are worth taking a closer look at. Models and exemplars are particularly important for educators who need to see and visit places where schooling is different. This is by no means a comprehensive list of deeper learning schools, and there are many other schools that we could have featured. But this selection offers a good representation of some of the diverse and interesting organizational and instructional models that are emerging around the world.

If there is an innovative school in your area that seems to be doing well on one or more of the four big shifts, let us know!

Iowa BIG, Cedar Rapids, Iowa

Arguably the most innovative school in Iowa, Iowa BIG has an interesting birth story. In 2012, the Cedar Rapids Community School District began inviting local business and political leaders to come back to school for a day (Education Reimagined, 2015). Each invitee shadowed a high school student in the morning and then spent lunch and the rest of the afternoon discussing what they saw. Following the visit, the district officials asked those local leaders what knowledge, skills, and dispositions were necessary for success in their organizations, and whether they had seen evidence of those qualities in the classes that they had attended. The local leaders highlighted and discussed several disconnects between what they'd seen in the school's metrics and students' learning experience and the factors they believed were necessary for success in the outside world.

After several rounds of these visits, the Cedar Rapids community finally asked: "Okay, what would a school look like that addressed these disconnects?" Thus, Iowa BIG was born.

Iowa BIG is centered around a community project pool. Local companies, non-profits, and city and county government agencies typically have wish lists of projects for which they don't have the personnel, time, or resources. They pitch these projects to the students at Iowa BIG, who then select two or three projects to work on at any given time. Half of the students' days are spent at their local, traditional high school—the *mothership*, as they call it. The other half are spent at Iowa BIG or out in the community working on projects, meeting with partners and mentors, making connections, or garnering needed information, funding, and resources.

Example student projects have included transforming the ailing local zoo into an interactive and educational urban farm, researching the evolution of grapes with a faculty member at the University of Northern Iowa, creating a one-handed keyboard for amputees, and helping an architecture firm redesign a local elementary school into a STEAM (science, technology, engineering, the arts, and mathematics) magnet school. Other projects have included developing a waterborne drone that measures plastic waste in riverways and oceans, designing arthritis-friendly utensils, creating a documentary of the county's first medical examiner, designing and testing an aquaponics system in North Africa, developing a recycling bin that tweets every item thrown into it, and initiating a young women's entrepreneurship community and annual conference.

As students work on their projects, their instructors act primarily as facilitators, guiding students toward necessary questions and resources as needed. As student work progresses, their teachers meet regularly to debrief the learning that is occurring for each student, identify what curriculum standards the student is meeting through the project (hint: students have to learn a lot of mathematics and science to get a drone to work), and award course credits as students accrue them. Everything is managed within Iowa BIG's homegrown, progress-monitoring database. And because Iowa BIG is strategically located in a building that houses a start-up company accelerator, students have access to adult entrepreneurs as well as to advice about how to create and protect any intellectual property that their work generates.

New Village Girls Academy, Los Angeles, California

New Village Girls Academy (NVGA, 2017) is the only all-girl public high school in the state of California. Based in Los Angeles, NVGA serves about 110 girls in a small handful of classrooms that circle a dusty courtyard and a few lunch tables. Essentially every girl at NVGA lives in conditions of poverty, and about half of the girls are pregnant or already parenting. Approximately 30 percent of the students live with foster parents or in institutional foster homes. Many of the students are English learners, and it is very common for the girls to have personal and family backgrounds of drug abuse, sexual abuse, physical abuse, self-harm, incarceration, and other success-limiting life factors.

The motto at NVGA is to "reimagine what's possible," and its essential mission is to get its girls back on track and to send as many as possible off to college and into productive careers. The school has an incredible track record of sending its graduates off to college and careers. It's also perhaps Scott's favorite school of any he's visited.

NVGA is a member of the Big Picture Learning network, which started with the famous Met school in Providence, Rhode Island, and later expanded to nearly fifty schools across the country as of this writing. Every Big Picture Learning school uses advisories, internships, outside mentors, and project-based learning opportunities to create local student-centered learning designs. At NVGA, every girl has four key pillars that support her success: (1) her advisory, (2) her internship, (3) her passion project, and (4) a schoolwide focus on mindfulness that helps her stay cognitively and emotionally centered amidst the turmoil that may constitute her nonschool life.

Projects at NVGA are centered around big, important, essential questions. For instance, a student's project on the oil industry might investigate questions such as: What would the world be like without oil? Is the intersection of politics and gas companies good or bad? and Is gas worth killing for? Another student's project on animal testing might ask questions such as: What constitutes animal cruelty? Should animals have the right to painkillers? and How can cosmetic companies ensure human safety without using animal testing? (Notice that these questions address very real issues in the world, likely to a much greater degree than the questions your local school asks its students.)

Twice a week, the students avail themselves of city transportation options and travel to their internship locations. Internship settings range widely depending on students' interests: they may range from the bicycle shop or vintage record store around the corner all the way up to the California Science Center, the Los Angeles Police Department, or a U.S. senator's office. Internships at NVGA are not meant to provide local organizations with free labor. Instead, they are intended to teach the students how to be managers, owners, and entrepreneurs. Each girl has the opportunity to engage in up to eight internships—one per semester—during her four years at NVGA. Many of the girls find that the combination of passion projects and internships allows them to discover new competencies, to gain new skills, and to find a future direction for their lives.

New Technology High School, Sioux Falls, South Dakota

Located in Sioux Falls, South Dakota, New Technology High School (2017; New Tech High, for short) is one of approximately 175 schools in the New Tech

Network, an organization that spans twenty-eight U.S. states, plus Australia. The three mantras at New Tech High are "Culture that empowers, teaching that engages, and technology that enables," and these manifest themselves throughout the school's activities.

With the exception of a few electives, all of the courses at New Tech High are team taught by pairs of teachers. Those course pairings may be more traditional, such as language arts and social studies or mathematics and science, or they might be a bit more unexpected, such as geometry and graphic design. Each course at New Tech High is divided into a series of group projects. Over the course of the academic year, these projects cover most of the essential curriculum standards and learning outcomes of the paired courses. Students typically work in groups of four and are given an intake document at the beginning of each project. Each group is responsible for figuring out what tasks are necessary to accomplish the project outcomes and for dividing up the work, establishing time lines and deadlines, and determining what learning is necessary for the group to be successful. Because the success of New Tech High depends on functional group work, the school has evolved several mechanisms that facilitate positive and productive group interactions and interdependencies. As a result, group work at New Tech High is far more fruitful than in most traditional schools, where student and parent complaints regarding inequitable workloads and unfair grading are often rampant.

Example projects that groups take on might include writing and staging a sixth act of *Macbeth*; interviewing local business owners and redesigning their logos, stationery, and websites; or creating a public advocacy campaign for the South Dakota Game, Fish, and Parks Department that encourages homeowners and businesses to employ native plants and grasses in their landscaping efforts. In addition to typical academic content, each project at New Tech High also incorporates some or all of the school's six Schoolwide Learning Outcomes (SLOs): (1) oral communication, (2) written communication, (3) critical thinking, (4) collaboration, (5) technological proficiency, and (6) work ethic. These SLOs represent characteristics of a successful graduate that the school is trying to foster above and beyond what high school courses typically require. To facilitate this, each of the SLOs has a common rubric that every teacher uses across all grade levels and subject areas. These common rubrics create a schoolwide consistency in expectations. For example, a student who must give an oral presentation to the community at the conclusion of a project knows exactly what that presentation's criteria for success are. After giving fifty to one hundred such public presentations over the course of a high school career, all judged against the same rubric, that student is likely to be an amazing public speaker.

Along with an academic content grade, grades for each of the SLOs are reported separately in the New Tech Network's custom-designed online grading and project management portal, allowing students, teachers, and parents to track where students need more development and assistance. New Tech High's intentional focus on these analytical and interpersonal skills helps facilitate student capabilities that other schools usually relegate to extracurricular activities.

Ao Tawhiti Unlimited Discovery, Christchurch, New Zealand

When you walk in the doors of the Ao Tawhiti Unlimited Discovery school (New Learning, n.d.), students are all over the place. Two girls might be sitting around a table, going over the script for their play and making plans to hire actors and actresses; to do set design, marketing, and publicity; and to stage the play at a local theater. A boy might be down the hall on the phone, raising funds so that he and his classmates can take surfing lessons to get them ready for the end-of-term surfing tournament that he has arranged and that the top surfer in New Zealand will judge. Another clump of students might be found sitting under a few desks, trying to decide the best approach for their upcoming *Iron Chef* competition. One girl might have been pulled aside, talking with a teacher about her upcoming visit to a local hospital as research for her brain cancer awareness campaign, inspired by her friend's mother who died of the affliction. Another boy might be deeply focused on his computer screen as he attempts to master his sixth straight digital animation project: he is getting quite good, exhibiting skills often not seen until university age. Several girls might be out in the garden, discussing the show notes for their next radio broadcast. Later in the afternoon, many of the older students might be working with a parent volunteer who is an artist, learning how to do watercolor paintings so that they can illustrate their nonfiction books for same-age peers. And before the day ends, the students might come together as a whole to discuss their latest plans for a community fair, which will raise funds for earthquake victims in Japan. This is a typical day—pretty impressive for a school that serves ages nine through thirteen.

Ao Tawhiti is organized around the concept that students can drive their own learning in powerful ways. Every six weeks, students identify a topic of their choosing—either alone, in pairs, or in small groups—and then work with a teacher facilitator to turn that topic into a useful project. Teachers have been deeply trained in how to be effective coaches and have regular conversations about how to fill in their students' knowledge and skills gaps that may arise along the way. Students check in regularly with their teachers to inform them of their progress, and every two weeks a formal write-up documents the steps that students have taken, their future plans, and an assessment of what students have learned. On any given day, some students may not be at the school because they are out in the community meeting with people and implementing their projects.

Ao Tawhiti explodes the idea that students must operate within very tight confines and restrictions in order to learn successfully. Instead, the school invests deeply in its faith in youth, structuring itself to provide its students with necessary supports while remaining out of their way. Although there is no set curriculum and although students choose what they learn and work on, students score quite adequately on the end-of-year national exam. More important, the result is an extraordinary group of young people who are thoughtful, incredibly capable, focused on community impact, and confident in their interactions with adults.

Surrey Academy of Innovative Learning, Surrey, British Columbia

The Surrey school district in British Columbia has a growing reputation for innovation. Although it is quite large at seventy-six thousand students, the district has been consistent in its pursuit of innovative learning practices. The Surrey Academy of Innovative Learning (SAIL) is one such example. At its core, SAIL focuses on giving voice and choice to students by designing flexible learning environments. It evolved from a home connect program designed to use blended, online learning to support students who didn't have success in a typical school setting. Many school districts offer such online programing for high school students, but SAIL serves K–12 students within its own district and beyond (SAIL, 2017).

SAIL's activities at the elementary level are particularly intriguing. As a blended learning environment, the basic format for elementary students is four days in school and one home learning day. For this to work, parents must sign off on the home component and agree to serve as teachers during the time at home. In some respects, this simply acknowledges the natural relationship that parents already have as their child's first teacher.

When students aren't learning at home, they study within a physical space that looks nothing like traditional classrooms. There are no desks at SAIL, no rows, no front of the room. Instead, the furniture moves according to the learning. This is done to enhance student agency and ownership. As one parent said, "Students here are honored for their creativity and interests."

SAIL recognizes that grade levels have been largely a construct of convenience for teachers and school systems. True learning communities, however, should focus on the needs of the learners. Therefore, students at SAIL are not grouped according to grade levels but according to expectations about what groupings will create the most effective learning communities.

The SAIL curriculum meets all of the province's learning requirements, but there is a special focus within the school on STEAM (science, technology, engineering, the arts, and mathematics). The school also emphasizes design, exploration, problem solving, and creative expression, creating an interdisciplinary focus that aligns well with the school's intent to distance itself from traditional schooling structures.

Enrollment in SAIL continues to grow, and the teachers there are excited about the future. They recognize that part of their mission is to continue to adapt learning environments and structures to meet evolving student needs. Removing some of the barriers of time, space, and content has empowered both students and teachers.

Other Deeper Learning Schools

In addition to the previously discussed deeper learning schools, there are a number of school networks that are trying to foster deeper learning across all of their schools. These include:

- The Asia Society Center for Global Education's International Studies Schools Network, http://asiasociety.org/international-studies -schools-network

- Big Picture Learning, www.bigpicturelearning.org

- ConnectEd California, www.connectedcalifornia.org

- EdVisions Schools, www.edvisions.com

- EL Education, https://eleducation.org

- Envision Education, www.envisionschools.org

- High Tech High, www.hightechhigh.org

- Independent Curriculum Group, http://independentcurriculum.org

- Internationals Network for Public Schools, http://internationalsnps.org

- New Tech Network, https://newtechnetwork.org

- New Visions for Public Schools, www.newvisions.org

- New York Performance Standards Consortium, http://performance assessment.org

There are well over five hundred schools and over a quarter of a million students across these networks. In addition to the networks listed here, other schools that focus on active learning, student agency, and deeper thinking include Sudbury,

Montessori, Reggio Emilia, Waldorf, and democratic schools, as well as a whole host of individually innovative schools from across the world.

When schools allow students to go beyond procedural regurgitation and engage in creative, collaborative critical thinking and problem solving, students become deeper learners and doers who can add value beyond what search engines, Siri, and YouTube can already do. When schools allow students to drive their own learning, engagement and motivation levels are high, and students clearly learn to become autonomous and self-directed learners who can reskill and adapt to a rapidly changing world. When schools allow students to engage with and contribute to the world outside of the school walls, they learn to become locally and globally active citizens of both their communities and of the planet at large. And when schools allow students to use digital learning tools in robust ways, they become digitally fluent and capable of effectively navigating our technology-suffused world. So let's ask ourselves: "How quickly can we get more of these schools up and running?"

Practical Steps and Strategies

- Begin connecting with the lesson plans, videos, student work products, strategic plans, protocols, evaluation reports, and other documents that are available on the websites of many of the deeper learning networks.

- Familiarize your community with the research from the Hewlett Foundation and the American Institutes for Research (see Zeiser et al., 2016; Zeiser et al., 2014) showing that deeper learning schools can be as or more successful than traditional schools on a variety of desired learning and organizational outcomes.

- Because many educators can't conceive it until they can see it, send teachers, administrators, and parents on site visits to deeper learning schools to see their practices in action. Be sure to include skeptics on the visitation team!

- Implement small-scale pilots of deeper learning practices, using the four big shifts and ten building blocks described in the introduction (page 4) to help guide your work.

- Identify internal educators who are already engaging in deeper learning practices, and create a plan to share their expertise and scale it throughout the school system.

Epilogue

We recognize that many other educational reformers offer rhetoric that's similar to ours. Indeed, many of the ill-guided educational reform measures that plague school policy arenas today—including implementing longer school days and calendars, mandatory summer school, and increased seat time and testing, which have resulted in reduced access to recess, electives, gifted and talented programs, and opportunities for student-driven exploration—are a result of well-intentioned attempts to remedy both perceived and actual shortcomings. Yet very few of our existing policy and practice reforms focus on substantively transforming the learning environment, and very few address the root causes of disengagement, inequity, and irrelevance. Most important, very few are grounded in any productive understanding of students' day-to-day learning experiences. Most educational reforms to date have not succeeded either because they have failed to accurately diagnose or address root causes or because they represent attempts to address those causes through tweaks and intensifications of existing policies rather than through wholesale redesign (Darling-Hammond, 1997; Martinez & McGrath, 2014). Our problem as educators and policymakers is that we don't think or act big enough.

What do we mean by that?

- If schools are to genuinely prepare graduates to compete in a technology-infused information landscape, they must stop acting as they did when learning and teaching primarily occurred in analog formats. Instead, schools must begin to immerse students in the use of digital tools and in the outside contexts that surround those tools, and schools must do this in deeper and more significant ways.

- If schools are to genuinely prepare graduates for a hyperconnected and hypercompetitive global innovation economy, they must stop emphasizing low-level content coverage. Instead, they must focus on interdisciplinary thinking, interpersonal skills, and technological fluency: the skills that allow individuals to offer value and differentiate themselves in digital marketplaces.

- If schools are to genuinely prepare graduates to be powerful lifelong learners, they must stop blocking mobile devices, digital environments, and online communities out of fear, nostalgia, or concerns about maintaining control. Instead, they must help students learn how to utilize these tools to foster powerful learning and extracurricular connections.

- If schools are to genuinely engage students in their learning rather than simply force them to comply with academic and attendance directives, they must move away from one-size-fits-all instructional models. Instead, they must find ways to make the learning opportunities students experience more relevant and personally authentic.

- If schools are to genuinely prepare innovators rather than "just tell me what to do" workers, they must stop disengaging students by using extrinsic punishments and rewards to govern classrooms. Instead, they must transform their learning spaces into the kinds of engaging environments of discovery, play, and intrinsic motivation that reward innovation.

- And if schools are to genuinely address equity issues so that no child is truly left behind, they must no longer be content to provide exclusive access to technology and rich, creative technology education to those students who have the most advantages. Instead, schools must find ways to enable robust digital learning for all students.

We know that these changes are daunting. We know that revolutions are scary. And yet at certain times they're necessary. Now is one of those times. There are hundreds and perhaps thousands of deeper learning schools worldwide that already are making these transformations and implementing the four big shifts outlined in the introduction (page 4): (1) higher-level thinking, (2) student agency, (3) authentic work, and (4) technology infusion. There's clear evidence, whether we use new metrics or traditional ones, that these different school models work. The challenge for all of us, then, is to use them as guidelines to improve ourselves and our institutions so that we can better meet the needs of the students we serve.

At this point, you may be wondering, "Okay, I agree with much of this. But now what? What do I do next?" If so, start asking yourself and your local school organizations these questions.

- "How many of the six main arguments for educational transformation has your school already responded to? For example, is your school working to make students information literate, or working to overcome barriers to digital access for traditionally disadvantaged groups? What evidence do you have?"

- "How many of your school's existing lessons, units, and other instructional activities are strong in all four of the big shifts outlined in the introduction? How about just three? Or even just two? How might you implement those strengths more broadly?"

- "If you haven't implemented any of the four shifts already, could you implement one next year, at least as a small-scale pilot? Which schools, teachers, and students might be ideal for your pilot? What evidence will you collect to measure its success? And if it is successful, how might you scale it up to reach other students, staff, and schools?"

  Critical!

- "Are there any organizations, schools, classrooms, or educators in your state that are doing well with these building blocks and that you might visit and learn from?" (Hint: Maybe one or more of the deeper learning networks we listed in chapter 7 [page 41] has a school near you.)

- "What aspects of your school, parent, and community culture might you need to address in order to optimize the success of your transformation efforts?"

- "What else could you do to start moving your classroom, school, or district toward a deeper learning model?"

We can't sit idly by waiting for retirement, making excuses, or hoping that someone else will take on the challenge. We owe it to our children and grandchildren, our nieces and nephews, our neighbors and friends, to make school different—and we owe it to them yesterday.

So, let's roll up our sleeves and begin to create the new, relevant, amazing learning environments that our students deserve. Are you in?

Stay in Touch!

Feel free to contact us at any time to talk through any ideas, questions, challenges, or concerns that you have after reading this book. Visit http://dangerouslyirrelevant.org to find Scott, and visit http://ideasandthoughts.org to connect with Dean. We look forward to hearing from you!

References and Resources

Amabile, T. M. (1998, September-October). How to kill creativity. *Harvard Business Review, 76*(5), 76–87, 186.

Anderson, C. (2009). *Free: The future of a radical price.* New York: Hyperion.

Autor, D. H. (2014). *Polanyi's paradox and the shape of employment growth.* Cambridge, MA: Massachusetts Institute of Technology. Accessed at http://economics.mit.edu /files/9835 on February 21, 2017.

Autor, D. H., & Price, B. (2013, June). *The changing task composition of the U.S. labor market: An update of Autor, Levy, and Murnane (2003).* Cambridge: Massachusetts Institute of Technology. Accessed at http://economics.mit.edu/files/9758 on February 21, 2017.

Azzam, A. M. (2007). Special report: Why students drop out. *Educational Leadership, 64*(7), 91–93. Accessed at www.ascd.org/publications/educational-leadership /apr07/vol64/num07/Why-Students-Drop-Out.aspx on January 3, 2015.

Bloom, B. S. (Ed.). (1956). *Taxonomy of educational objectives: The classification of educational goals; Handbook I: Cognitive domain.* New York: Longmans.

Boser, U. (2013, June 14). *Are schools getting a big enough bang for their education technology buck?* Washington, DC: Center for American Progress. Accessed at www.americanprogress.org/issues/education/report/2013/06/14/66485/are -schools-getting-a-big-enough-bang-for-their-education-technology-buck on February 21, 2017.

Bowen, J. A. (2012). *Teaching naked: How moving technology out of your college classroom will improve student learning.* San Francisco: Jossey-Bass.

boyd, d. (2014). *It's complicated: The social lives of networked teens.* New Haven, CT: Yale University Press.

Bracey, G. (2009). The big tests: What ends do they serve? *Educational Leadership, 67*(3), 32–37.

Brown, E. (2015, October 28). U.S. student performance slips on national test. *The Washington Post.* Accessed at www.washingtonpost.com/local/education/us -student-performance-slips-on-national-test/2015/10/27/03c80170-7cb9-11e5 -b575-d8dcfedb4ea1_story.html?utm_term=.f4521cf54d81 on February 21, 2017.

Brynjolfsson, E., & McAfee, A. (2011). *Race against the machine: How the digital revolution is accelerating innovation, driving productivity, and irreversibly transforming employment and the economy.* Lexington, MA: Digital Frontier Press.

Bureau of Labor Statistics. (2016). *Employment, hours, and earnings from the Current Employment Statistics survey (national).* Washington, DC: Author. Accessed at http://data.bls.gov/ces on July 31, 2017.

Business RoundTable. (2005). *Tapping America's potential: The education for innovation initiative.* Washington, DC: Author. Accessed at http://tapcoalition.org/resource /pdf/TAP_report2.pdf on March 29, 2017.

Busteed, B. (2013, January 7). *The school cliff: Student engagement drops with each school year* [Blog post]. Accessed at www.gallup.com/opinion/gallup/170525 /school-cliff-student-engagement-drops-school-year.aspx on October 10, 2014.

Common Sense Media. (2017). *Digital citizenship.* Accessed at www.commonsense .org/education/digital-citizenship on June 3, 2017.

Couros, G. (2014, March 14). *Would you want to be a learner in your own classroom?* [Blog post]. Accessed at http://georgecouros.ca/blog/archives/4480 on February 21, 2017.

Darling-Hammond, L. (1997). *The right to learn: A blueprint for creating schools that work.* San Francisco: Jossey-Bass.

Dewey, J. (1916). *Democracy and education: An introduction to the philosophy of education.* New York: Macmillan.

Dyer, J. H., Gregersen, H., & Christensen, C. M. (2009). The innovator's DNA. *Harvard Business Review.* Accessed at https://hbr.org/2009/12/the-innovators-dna on February 21, 2017.

Education Reimagined. (2015, December 11). Iowa BIG. *Pioneering* (3), 5–8. Accessed at http://go.shr.lc/2qUrRmH on June 3, 2017.

EdVisions Schools. (2009). *Proven results.* Henderson, MN: Author. Accessed at http://edvisions.com/goto/Proven_Results on June 3, 2017.

Eisenberg, M. B., Berkowitz, R. E., Jansen, B. A., & Little, T. J. (1999). *Teaching information and technology skills: The Big6 in elementary schools.* Columbus, OH: Linworth.

EL Education. (2016). *EL Education by the numbers.* Accessed at http://eleducation .org/results/by-the-numbers on February 21, 2017.

Elmore, R. F. (2006). *Education leadership as the practice of improvement.* Keynote presentation given at the Annual Convention of the University Council for Educational Administration, San Antonio, TX. Accessed at http://www.scott mcleod.org/2006UCEAElmore.mp3 on March 29, 2017.

Ferla, A. (2011). *Putting the new GM-UAW contract in historical context.* Accessed at www.remappingdebate.org/map-data-tool/putting-new-gm-uaw-contract -historical-context on March 29, 2017.

Florida, R. (2002). *The rise of the creative class: And how it's transforming work, leisure, community, and everyday life.* New York: Basic Books.

Frey, C. B., & Osborne, M. A. (2013). *The future of employment: How susceptible are jobs to computerization?* Oxford, England: University of Oxford. Accessed at www.oxfordmartin.ox.ac.uk/publications/view/1314 on February 21, 2017.

Fried, R. L. (2005). *The game of school: Why we all play it, how it hurts kids, and what it will take to change it.* San Francisco: Jossey-Bass.

Future Ready Schools. (2015). *Future ready framework.* Accessed at http://futureready .org/about-the-effort/framework on June 3, 2017.

Gallup. (2016). *Gallup student poll: Engaged today—Ready for tomorrow.* Accessed at http://kidsathope.org/wp-content/uploads/2015/05/2015-Gallup-Student-Poll -Overall-Report.pdf on February 21, 2017.

Godin, S. (2012). *Stop stealing dreams (What is school for?).* Accessed at www.sethgodin .com/sg/docs/stopstealingdreamsscreen.pdf on February 21, 2017.

Goodlad, J. I. (1984). *A place called school: Prospects for the future.* New York: McGraw-Hill.

Heitner, D. (2016). *Screenwise: Helping kids thrive (and survive) in their digital world.* New York: Routledge.

Hewlett Foundation. (2017). *Deeper learning.* Accessed at http://www.hewlett.org /strategy/deeper-learning on June 3, 2017.

High Tech High. (2015). *Results.* Accessed at www.hightechhigh.org/about/results.php on January 15, 2015.

Horowitz, S. (2015). *This is what the state of freelancing in the U. S. means for the future of work.* Accessed at www.fastcompany.com/3051686/the-future-of-work/the -state-of-freelancing-in-the-us-in-2015 on February 21, 2017.

International Association for K–12 Online Learning. (2015). *Blending learning: The evolution of online and face-to-face education from 2008–2015.* Accessed at http://files.eric.ed.gov/fulltext/ED560788.pdf on March 29, 2017.

International Society for Technology in Education. (2017a). *Essential conditions.* Accessed at www.iste.org/standards/tools-resources/essential-conditions on June 3, 2017.

International Society for Technology in Education. (2017b). *Lead & transform diagnostic tool.* Accessed at www.iste.org/standards/tools-resources/lead-transform /diagnostic-tool on June 3, 2017.

Ito, M., Baumer, S., Bittani, M., boyd, d., Cody, R., Herr-Stephenson, B., et al. (2010). *Hanging out, messing around, and geeking out: Kids living and learning with new media.* Cambridge, MA: MIT Press.

Jarvis, J. (2009). *What would Google do?* New York: Collins Business.

Jenkins, H. (2006). *Convergence culture: Where old and new media collide.* New York: New York University Press.

Kamenetz, A. (2016, October 12). *The high school graduation rate reaches a record high—again.* Washington, DC: National Public Radio. Accessed at www.npr.org /sections/ed/2016/10/17/498246451/the-high-school-graduation-reaches-a -record-high-again on July 18. 2017.

Lankshear, C., & Knobel, M. (2011). *New literacies: Everyday practices and social learning* (3rd ed.). Maidenhead, England: Open University Press.

Levine, R., Locke, C., Searls, D., & Weinberger, D. (2000). *The cluetrain manifesto: The end of business as usual.* Cambridge, MA: Perseus Books.

Levy, F., & Murnane, R. J. (2004). *The new division of labor: How computers are creating the next job market.* Princeton, NJ: Princeton University Press.

Margolis, J. (2014). Hybrid teacher leaders and the new professional development ecology. In A. Alexandrou & S. Swaffield (Eds.), *Teacher leadership and professional development* (pp. 129–153). New York: Routledge.

Martinez, M. R., & McGrath, D. (2014). *Deeper learning: How eight innovative public schools are transforming education in the twenty-first century.* New York: New Press.

Maslow, A. H. (1943). A theory of human motivation. *Psychological Review, 50*(4), 370–396.

McLeod, S. (n.d.). *Trudacot.* Accessed at http://dangerouslyirrelevant.org/resources /trudacot on June 5, 2017.

McLeod, S. (2014, December 22). We need schools to be different. *The Huffington Post.* Accessed at www.huffingtonpost.com/scott-mcleod/we-need-schools-to-be -dif_b_6353198.html on June 28, 2016.

Merrow, J. (2012, September 17). *Blended learning, but to what end?* [Blog post]. Accessed at http://takingnote.learningmatters.tv/?p=5908 on February 21, 2017.

Moscaritolo, A. (2013, October 3). LA confiscates student iPads over unauthorized app use. *PC Magazine.* Accessed at http://in.pcmag.com/tablets/69904/news/la -confiscates-student-ipads-over-unauthorized-app-use on February 21, 2017.

Mouly, V. S., & Sankaran, J. K. (2002). The enactment of envy within organizations: Insights from a New Zealand academic department. *The Journal of Applied Behavioral Science, 38*(1), 36–56.

National Academy of Science. (2007). *Rising above the gathering storm: Energizing and employing America for a brighter economic future.* Washington, DC: Author.

National Commission on Excellence in Education. (1983). *A nation at risk: The imperative for educational reform.* Washington, DC: Author. Accessed at https://www2.ed.gov/pubs/NatAtRisk/risk.html on March 15, 2017.

National Council of Teachers of English. (2013). *NCTE framework for 21st century curriculum and assessment.* Urbana, IL: Author. Accessed at http://www.ncte.org /library/NCTEFiles/Resources/Positions/Framework_21stCent_Curr _Assessment.pdf on March 28, 2017.

New Commission on the Skills of the American Workforce. (2006). *Tough choices or tough times.* Washington, DC: National Center on Education and the Economy.

New Learning. (n.d.). *Discovery 1, Christchurch.* Accessed at http://newlearningonline .com/new-learning/chapter-2/discovery-1-christchurch on June 3, 2017.

New Tech Network. (2015). *2015 New Tech Network student outcomes report.* Napa, CA: Author. Accessed at https://32dkl02ezpk0qcqvqmlx19lk-wpengine.netdna-ssl.com /wp-content/uploads/2016/08/newtechnetwork2015studentoutcomesreport.pdf on March 28, 2017.

New Technology High School. (2017). *New Technology High School.* Accessed at www.sf.k12.sd.us/schools/high-schools/new-technology on June 3, 2017.

New Village Girls Academy. (2017). *New Village Girls Academy.* Accessed at https://new villagegirlsacademy.org on June 3, 2017.

O'Rourke, M. (2005, May). *Multiliteracies for 21st century schools.* Strawberry Hills, New South Wales: Australian National Schools Network.

Perkins, D. N. (2014). *Future wise: Educating our children for a changing world.* San Francisco: Jossey-Bass.

Pianta, R. C., Belsky, J., Houts, R., & Morrison, F. (2007). Opportunities to learn in America's elementary classrooms. *Science, 315*(5820), 1795–1796.

Postman, N., & Weingartner, C. (1969). *Teaching as a subversive activity.* New York: Delacorte Press.

Prensky, M. (2008). Turning on the lights. *Educational Leadership, 65*(6), 40–45.

Ravitch, D. (2003). *The language police: How pressure groups restrict what students learn.* New York: Vintage Books.

Reich, J. (2013, June 14). Shockingly similar digital divide findings from 1998 and 2013 [Editorial]. *Education Week.* Accessed at http://blogs.edweek.org /edweek/edtechresearcher/2013/06/shockingly_similar_digital_divide_findings _from_1998_and_2013.html on March 29, 2017.

Resnick, L. B. (1987). *Education and learning to think.* Washington, DC: National Academies Press.

Rich, M. (2013, June 13). Study gauges value of technology in schools. *New York Times,* p. A17.

Richardson, W. (2012). *Why school? How education must change when learning and information are everywhere.* New York: TED Books.

Rideout, V., & Katz, V. S. (2016). *Opportunity for all? Technology and learning in lower-income families.* New York: The Joan Ganz Cooney Center at Sesame Workshop.

Rothstein, D., & Santana, L. (2011). *Make just one change: Teach students to ask their own questions.* Cambridge, MA: Harvard Education Press.

Scarfe, N. V. (1962). Play is education. *Childhood Education, 39*(3), 117–120.

Schlechty Center. (2012, April 5). *The role of the teacher is changing* [Video file]. Accessed at www.youtube.com/watch?v=15rs4y4PvKE on March 28, 2017.

Schmoker, M. (2006). *Results now: How we can achieve unprecedented improvements in teaching and learning.* Alexandria, VA: Association for Supervision and Curriculum Development.

Shareski, D. (2009). *The school bus.* Accessed at www.flickr.com/photos/shareski /4209837879 on June 3, 2017.

Standage, T. (2013). *Writing on the wall: Social media—The first 2,000 years.* London: Bloomsbury.

Surrey Academy of Innovative Learning. (2017). *Our school.* Accessed at https:// sailacademy.ca/about on June 3, 2017.

Thomas, D., & Brown, J. S. (2011). *A new culture of learning: Cultivating the imagination for a world of constant change.* Lexington, KY: CreateSpace Independent Publishing Platform.

Valentine, J. (2005, August). *The instructional practices inventory: A process for profiling student engaged learning for school improvement.* Columbia, MO: Middle Level Leadership Center.

Wagner, T. (2008). *The global achievement gap: Why even our best schools don't teach the new survival skills our children need—and what we can do about it.* New York: Basic Books.

Wagner, T. (2012a). *Creating innovators: The making of young people who will change the world.* New York: Scribner.

Wagner, T. (2012b, May 30). *Play, passion, purpose: Tony Wagner at TEDxNYED* [Video file]. Accessed at www.youtube.com/watch?v=hvDjh4l-VHo on March 28, 2017.

Watters, A. (2013, October 2). Students are "hacking" their school-issued iPads: Good for them. *The Atlantic.* Accessed at www.theatlantic.com/technology/archive /2013/10/students-are-hacking-their-school-issued-ipads-good-for-them/280196 on February 21, 2017.

Webb, N. L. (2002). *Depth-of-knowledge levels for four content areas.* Accessed at http://facstaff.wcer.wisc.edu/normw/All%20content%20areas%20%20 DOK%20levels%2032802.pdf on April 21, 2017.

Wenglinsky, H. (1998). *Does it compute? The relationship between educational technology and student achievement in mathematics.* Princeton, NJ: Educational Testing Service.

Wilocis. (2016). *MOOC list.* Accessed at www.mooc-list.com on June 3, 2017.

Wolf, G. (1996, February 1). *Steve Jobs: The next insanely great thing.* Accessed at www.wired.com/1996/02/jobs-2 on June 3, 2017.

Yang, D. (2016). A year of change for employment, culture, and education in 2016. *The Huffington Post.* Accessed at www.huffingtonpost.com/dennis-yang/a-year-of -change-for-employment_b_8913260.html on March 29, 2017.

Zeiser, K. L., Mills, N., Wulach, S., & Garet, M. S. (2016, March). *Graduation advantage persists for students in deeper learning network high schools: Updated findings from the Study of Deeper Learning—Opportunities and outcomes.* Washington, DC: American Institutes for Research.

Zeiser, K. L., Taylor, J., Rickles, J., Garet, M. S., & Segeritz, M. (2014). *Evidence of deeper learning outcomes: Findings from the Study of Deeper Learning— Opportunities and outcomes.* Washington, DC: American Institutes for Research.

Solutions for Creating the Learning Spaces Students Deserve

Solutions Series: Solutions for Creating the Learning Spaces Students Deserve reimagines the norms defining K–12 education. In a short, reader-friendly format, these books challenge traditional thinking about schooling and encourage readers to question their beliefs about what real teaching and learning look like in action.

Creating a Culture of Feedback
William M. Ferriter and Paul J. Cancellieri
BKF731

Embracing a Culture of Joy
Dean Shareski
BKF730

Making Learning Flow
John Spencer
BKF733

Reimagining Literacy Through Global Collaboration
Pernille Ripp
BKF732

Wait! Your professional development journey doesn't have to end with the last pages of this book.

We realize improving student learning doesn't happen overnight. And your school or district shouldn't be left to puzzle out all the details of this process alone.

No matter where you are on the journey, we're committed to helping you get to the next stage.

Take advantage of everything from **custom workshops** to **keynote presentations** and **interactive web and video conferencing**. We can even help you develop an action plan tailored to fit your specific needs.

Let's get the conversation started.

Call 888.763.9045 today.

SolutionTree.com